RICHARD J. FOSTER'S
STUDY GUIDE TO
MONEY, SEX & POWER

RICHARD J. FOSTER'S STUDY GUIDE TO MONEY, SEX & POWER

Richard J. Foster

1817

Harper & Row, Publishers, San Francisco

Cambridge, Hagerstown, New York, Philadelphia
London, Mexico City, São Paulo, Singapore, Sydney

A STUDY GUIDE TO MONEY, SEX & POWER. Copyright © 1985 by Richard J. Foster. All rights reserved. Printed in the United States of America. No part of this book may be used or reproduced in any manner whatsoever without written permission except in the case of brief quotations embodied in critical articles and reviews. For information address Harper & Row, Publishers, Inc., 10 East 53rd Street, New York, NY 10022. Published simultaneously in Canada by Fitzhenry & Whiteside, Limited, Toronto.

FIRST EDITION

Library of Congress Cataloging-in-Publication Data

Foster, Richard J.
    Richard J. Foster's Study guide to money, sex & power.

    1. Economics—Religious aspects—Christianity.
    2. Marriage—Religious aspects—Christianity.
    3. Authority—Moral and ethical aspects.   I. Title.
    II. Title: Study guide to money, sex & power.
HB72.F66   1985   248.4'896   84-48785
ISBN 0-06-062827-8

89   MPC   10   9   8   7   6   5   4

In memory of David M. Leach

*faithful minister of Christ and
dear friend to our family*

Contents

PART III. POWER

Preface: About This Study Guide

My hope in writing this *Study Guide* is to provide you with resources to further the discussion of the book *Money, Sex & Power*. Although I trust it will be helpful, I want to emphasize that it is only supplemental and not intended to replace a serious reading of the book itself. Each chapter begins with five brief Readings. This will give you the opportunity to sample, however briefly, the wealth of writings we have at our disposal. Many faithful Christian leaders over the centuries have written thoughtfully on these most contemporary of issues. Each reading should stimulate profitable discussion.

The Daily Scripture Readings allow you to meditate on the chapter topic in light of the biblical witness. Many other passages could be added, and you may want to develop a biblical study of your own on one of the topics that interests you.

The Study Questions are meant to stimulate thought and discussion. The many issues raised in *Money, Sex & Power* are vitally important and exceedingly difficult. I would be genuinely surprised (and concerned) if those issues did not stimulate lively debate. If the questions can help sharpen that debate, they have served their purpose.

The object of the "Creative Serendipities" is to encourage movement from discussion about the topic to experience of the topic. "Head" religion is not enough—

we must learn to descend with the head into the heart. The serendipities are best experienced in a group but can be done individually. If the suggestions that I have made do not fit your context, you can easily develop serendipities of your own.

A word needs to be said about the books listed at the end of each section. I decided that it would be most helpful to provide a listing broad enough to give you some sense of what is in the field. Consequently, the books listed express many different viewpoints, some of them decidedly opposed to the Christian position. For this reason, I have made evaluative statements about the books in the annotations. In every case I have sought to be both honest and kind. Of all people, Christians can most risk interacting with those of differing positions, for we know that the truth is greater than our defense of it.

Richard J. Foster
February 1985
Friends University

Chapter 1 Money, Sex and Power in Christian Perspective

We live in a secular world, but let us look at money, sex, and power from a Christian viewpoint.

READINGS

ON CONTROLLING DESIRE

Whenever a man longs for anything beyond measure immediately he is disturbed within. The proud and the covetous are never at rest. The poor and the humble in spirit live in the fulness of peace.

—Thomas à Kempis*

THE VOCATION OF EVERY MAN AND WOMAN

Biblical poverty, chastity and obedience are the vocation of every man and woman, and they are, I hope I have indicated, our way to authentic humanity. It must be so, as through such a life-style we follow the poor, chaste and obedient Jesus of Nazareth along a path which leads to the ultimate answer to the deepest longings of the hearts of all men and women: resurrection.

—Francis Moloney

---

* Sources for Readings can be found beginning on p. 111.

ANGER, MONEY AND SEX

During recent years several persons from The Church of the Saviour have worked in various group processes exploring and developing ways of working creatively with three vital areas of the Inward Journey—anger, money and sex. They have asked, How can we, as Christians, deal with these emotion-laden areas which are so often destructive and restricting to turn them into positive, lifegiving areas of new freedom, love and creative energy for healing? . . . Contemporizing the old monastic vows of Poverty, Chastity and Obedience for each of us is indeed life-giving and freeing.

—Donald D. McClanen

A TRULY SUPERNATURAL SELF-DENIAL

But the Holy Spirit also teaches the difference between asceticism and sacrifice, and shows us that for a Christian asceticism is not enough. Asceticism is content systematically to mortify and control our nature. Sacrifice does something more: it offers our nature and all its faculties to God. A self-denial that is truly supernatural must aspire to offer God what we have renounced ourselves.

—Thomas Merton

A PRAYERFUL LIFE

The pursuit of a prayerful life of simple love and discipleship sets us in isolation from and opposition to the mainstream, mammon-directed culture in which we live. We become deserters from technocracy, disaffiliating ourselves from its power, rejecting its false values. To pray is to drop out in the most profound and positive sense.

—Kenneth Leech

DAILY SCRIPTURE READINGS

STUDY QUESTIONS

1. Has the Church today given adequate, or inadequate, instruction on the issues of money, sex, and power? Are there historical factors that account for this?

2. Historically, the interrelatedness of money, sex, and power is easy to see. Have you observed this phenomenon in your world—that is, business, school, and so on?

3. In a recent television talk show with Marshall Loeb (managing editor of *Money* magazine) and Dr. Joyce Brothers (well-known psychologist), it was suggested that sex was the issue of the 1960s and 70s, money is the issue of the 80s, and power will be the issue of the 90s. What do you think?

4. I write, "Historically it seems spiritual revivals have been accompanied by a clear, bold response to the issues of money, sex, and power." What do you think? What implications for the Church today flow from such an idea?

5. I suggest that the social dimensions of money, sex, and power are business, marriage, and government. See if you or your group can come up with three action steps for each category that would bring these areas of life more fully into obedience to the way of Christ.

6. Of the monastic vows of poverty, chastity, and obedience, which do you think is the most defensible biblically? The least?

7. I write that the monastics "renounced possessions in order to learn detachment. They renounced marriage in order to learn vacancy. They renounced power in order to learn service." What are some ways that those of us who have not taken the monastic vows can learn about detachment, vacancy, and service?

8. What did you like in the Puritan emphasis upon industry, faithfulness, and order? What did you dislike?

9. The monastic movement and the Puritan movement are two groups that have worked on the money-sex-power issue. What are some other groups? What contribution did they make?

10. Given the church and world scene today, do you think it is important to have a new articulation of Christian "vows"? What practical difference could such a concept make in your church?

CREATIVE SERENDIPITIES

SERENDIPITY #1

"Create in me a clean heart, O God, and renew a right spirit within me" (Ps. 51:10, KJV).

Have someone read Psalm 51 out loud. (This psalm is David's cry of repentance over his affair with Bathsheba.)

Now silently, inwardly picture a hallway with three doors that open into three rooms in your life. The doors

4

are labeled, respectively; money, sex, power. You invite Jesus Christ to enter each room and in his loving way to show you things that need to be confessed. You readily confess them, for you sense his greater readiness to forgive them, each one.

Do not rush the process. Rather, be still and quiet until you have dealt with each item. If this is being done in a group, allow for a full fifteen to twenty minutes to pass in complete silence. Conclude with the strong words of 1 John 1:9 spoken out loud: "If we confess our sins, he is faithful and just, and will forgive our sins and cleanse us from all unrighteousness."

SERENDIPITY #2

"Lift up your hands to the holy place, and bless the LORD!" (Ps. 134:2). Read Psalm 134 out loud; if you are in a group, read it in unison.

Now lift your hands and bless God. Thank him! Praise him! Rejoice in his goodness! Remember, he has made heaven and earth, and what he has made is good.

Thank him, bless him for money:

—money to provide food, shelter, clothing

—money to bless the poor and needy

—money to extend his kingdom upon the earth

Thank him, bless him for sex:

—for your faithful marriage partner

—for intimacy and tenderness

—for a sexuality that helps define who we are

Thank him, bless him for power:

—power to turn away from the dangerous network of domination and manipulation of our dark world

—power to love and serve

—power to heal and help

Whether alone or in a group, close by singing:

All hail the power of Jesus' name!
Let angels prostrate fall;
Bring forth the royal diadem,
And crown Him Lord of all
Bring forth the royal diadem,
And crown Him Lord of all!

BOOKS ON GENERAL BACKGROUND

The books in this section are organized into the following categories:

The Devotional Masters

The Monastic Vows

Puritan Thought

Contemporary Analysis

THE DEVOTIONAL MASTERS

Arnold, Eberhard, ed. *The Early Christians: A Sourcebook on the Witness of the Early Church.* Grand Rapids, Mich.: Baker Book House, 1979. (A good collection of passages, mainly from the early church fathers, that would not be available to the average reader. It covers a variety of subjects and does give passages on the subjects of money and power.)

Augustine. *The Confessions of Saint Augustine.* Trans. by Rex Warner. New York: New American Library of World Literature, 1963. (The classic autobiography by one of the most influencial Christians of all time. Throughout *The Confessions* considerable attention is given to the questions of money, sex, and power.)

Bonhoeffer, Dietrich. *The Cost of Discipleship.* New York: Macmillan, 1963. (This book simply cannot be neglected by disciples today. Its influence has been immense; for example, it is the book that gave us the phrase "cheap grace." His chapter "The Simplicity of the Carefree Life" is worth the entire book. Read it all, however, for it frames the basis from which a serious response to money, sex, and power can be launched.)

Brother Ugolino di Monte Santa Maria. *The Little Flowers of St. Francis.* Trans. by Raphael Brown. Garden City, N.Y.: Image Books, 1958. (Delightful stories of the early Franciscans that give numerous insights into their perceptions on money, sex, and power.)

Colliander, Tito. *Way of the Ascetics.* Trans. by Katharine Ferré. San Francisco: Harper & Row, 1960. (This is a good book to introduce modern readers to the Eastern Christian spiritual tradition. It gives counsel in the spiritual life with warmth and common sense. There are specific chapters on money and power.)

Woolman, John. *The Journal of John Woolman and A Plea for the Poor.* Secaucus, N.J.: Citadel Press, 1972. (Perhaps the most contemporary of the classical spiritual journals because of the issues it faces. Throughout are significant reflections on power and money. It is a book well worth reading.

THE MONASTIC VOWS

Athanasius. *The Life of Antony and the Letter to Marcellinus.* Trans. by Robert C. Gregg. New York: Paulist Press, 1980. (This biography by Athanasius in the fourth century of his older contemporary, Antony [known as Anthony], quickly gained the status of a classic. It won acclaim, not only among Greek-speaking Christians in the eastern Mediterranean, but also among Latin Christians in Gaul and Italy. One modern scholar noted that by A.D. 400 Antony "was already a hero of the past." This rather instant notoriety ["instant" by ancient, not contemporary, standards] is largely due to Athanasius' *Vita Antonii.* Antony, of course, is known as the father of monasticism, and this engaging story of his life by an admirer and contemporary is an invaluable aid in understanding the monastic response to the money-sex-power issue.)

Fry, Timothy, ed. *The Rule of St. Benedict.* Collegeville, Minn.: Liturgical Press, 1981. (An excellent history of the Benedictine order, with a new translation of the Rule of St. Benedict and an expanded commentary upon it.)

Holmes, Urban T., III. *Spirituality for Ministry.* San Francisco: Harper & Row, 1982. (Attempts to think through the concepts of poverty, chastity, and obedience outside of a monastic world and within the context of contemporary life. Cumbersome reading but worth the effort.)

Moloney, Francis J. *A Life of Promise: Poverty, Chastity, Obedience*. Wilmington, Del.: Michael Glazier, 1984. (A modern attempt to think through the meaning of the monastic vows of poverty, chastity, and obedience.)

O'Reilly, James. *Lay and Religious States of Life: Their Distinction and Complementarity*. Chicago: Franciscan Herald Press, 1976. (A Catholic look at poverty, chastity, and obedience, with a strong emphasis upon making a clear demarcation between lay and religious states of life.)

Williams, H. A. *Poverty, Chastity & Obedience: The True Virtues*. London: Mitchell Beazley, 1975. (Four addresses given at Cambridge University that attempt to show the value of monastic vows for life today.)

Workman, Herbert B. *The Evolution of the Monastic Ideal*. London: Charles H. Kelly, 1913. (For those interested, this will provide good historical background on the monastic vows. It is a reverent and usually sympathetic treatment.)

PURITAN THOUGHT

Baxter, Richard. *Chapters from "A Christian Directory."* Edited by Jeanette Tawney. London: G. Bell & Sons, 1925. (One of the finest examples of Puritan thought, particularly on the subjects of money and power. Contains chapters titled "Directions for the Rich," "Directions for the Poor," "The Duties of Servants to Their Masters," etc.)

Bremer, Francis J. *The Puritan Experiment*. New York: St. Martin's Press, 1976. (Helpful background material on the Puritan efforts to establish a "Christian society" in New England. Particularly helpful chapters on the Puritan doctrine of the church and of the state.)

Foster, Stephen. *Their Solitary Way*. New Haven, Conn.: Yale University Press, 1971. (A study of Puritan thinking with special attention given to wealth and government. Helps to give a more balanced understanding of Puritan thinking.)

Frost, J. William. *The Quaker Family in Colonial America*. New York: St. Martin's Press, 1973. (An interesting look at how Quakers in the Colonial period sought to relate to sex and marriage issues. It surveys, for example, many of the early Quaker tracts and epistles on how one should select a wife or husband. I place it under Puritan thought because Quakers could rightly be considered the left wing of the Puritan revolt.)

Haller, William. *The Rise of Puritanism*. New York: Harper & Brothers, 1957. (Helpful background material on this important Christian movement.)

Hambrick-Stowe, Charles E. *The Practice of Piety*. Chapel Hill, N.C.: University of North Carolina Press, 1982. (Helpful material on the Puritan life-style, especially emphasizing its devotional and contemplative character.)

Knappen, M. M. *Tudor Puritanism: A Chapter in the History of Idealism*. Chicago: University of Chicago Press, 1939. (Helpful background material on English Puritanism. Contains a chapter entitled "The Puritan Doctrine of Authority" and one entitled "Domestic Life.")

Miller, Perry. *The New England Mind*. 2 vols. Cambridge, Mass.: Harvard University Press, 1954. (Written by one of the foremost authorities on the Puritans. It contains three excellent chapters on the covenant of grace, the visible or church covenant, and the social covenant.)

Miller, Perry, and Thomas H. Johnson, eds. *The Puritans: A Sourcebook of Their Writings*. 2 vols., rev. New York: Harper & Row, 1963. (This two-volume work is an excellent way to get at primary source material from the Puritans themselves. The bibliographical material and index in the back are rich sources for further study.)

Morgan, Edmund S. *The Puritan Family: Religion & Domestic Relations in Seventeenth-Century New England*. New York: Harper & Row, Rev. 1966. (A very readable and helpful book on the Puritan family structure. It shows the keen interest of Puritans upon effective and successful family life.)

———. "The Puritans and Sex." *The New England Quarterly*, Dec. 1942, pp. 591–607. (Explodes the common notion that Puritans held unhealthy taboos regarding sex. Written by one of the foremost authorities on Puritanism.)

———. *Visible Saints: The History of a Puritan Idea*. New York: New York University Press, 1963. (Helpful material on the Puritan doctrine of ecclesiology, particularly their emphasis upon a pure church and the visible covenant.)

Rutman, Darrett B. *American Puritanism: Faith and Practice*. New York: J. B. Lippincott, 1970. (A good background summary of Puritans in the New World for those who have little historical knowledge of the Puritans.)

Ryken, Leland. "Puritan Work Ethic: The Dignity of Life's Labors." *Christianity Today*, 19 Oct. 1979, pp. 15–18. (A very succinct and helpful article on the Puritan stance toward work.)

Schneider, Herbert Wallace. *The Puritan Mind*. New York: Henry Holt, 1930. (Contains a chapter, "The Holy Commonwealth," that helps to flesh out the Puritan doctrine of the state.)

Silverman, Kenneth. *The Life and Times of Cotton Mather*. New York: Harper & Row, 1984. (Probably the finest modern biography of a great American Puritan.)

Simpson, Alan. *Puritanism in Old and New England*. Chicago: University of Chicago Press, 1955. (A brief little book that gives a helpful summary of the Puritan concept of the visible covenant.)

Waller, George M., ed. *Puritanism in Early America*. 2d ed. Lexington, Mass.: D. C. Heath, 1973. (Several excellent chapters on the Puritan view of power and authority.)

Watkins, Owen C. *The Puritan Experience*. New York: Schocken Books, 1972. (An interesting study of Puritan life through their spiritual autobiographies. Of particular interest is his attempt to show the debt Quakerism owes to the Puritan movement.)

Wertenbaker, Thomas Jefferson. *The Puritan Oligarchy*. New York: Scribner's, 1947. (Provides historical background, especially in considering the Puritan use of order in government as a way to answer the power question.)

CONTEMPORARY ANALYSIS

Dostoevsky, Fyodor. *The Idiot*. Trans. by Constance Garnett. New York: Bantam Books, 1981. (In this magnificent novel, Dostoevsky places his Christ-figure, Prince Myshkin, into the heart of a society obsessed with wealth, power, and sexual conquest. Throughout the novel Dostoevsky is trying to show how a truly "beautiful soul" deals with the issues of money, sex, and power.)

Ellul, Jacques. *The Ethics of Freedom*. Trans. and edited by Geoffrey W. Bromiley. Grand Rapids, Mich.: Eerdmans, 1976. (An important treatment of ethical considerations by a first-rate Christian author. Contains sections entitled "Freedom in Relation to the Powers" and "Freedom in the Family, Work, Sex, and Money.")

Fawcett, Edmund, and Tony Thomas. *The American Condition*. New York: Harper & Row, 1982. (An analysis of contemporary

American culture, with chapters dealing with the economy, the family, and government, i.e., the social dimensions of money, sex, and power.)

Kraybill, Donald B. *The Upside-Down Kingdom*. Scottsdale, Penn.: Herald Press, 1978. (Very helpful in giving a perspective on the kingdom of God, with exceptionally good chapters on the money and power questions. Very readable.)

Naisbitt, John. *Megatrends: Ten New Directions Transforming Our Lives.* New York: Warner Books, 1984. (Helps us to think through the general movement of modern culture.)

Nouwen, Henri J. M. *The Wounded Healer*. Garden City, N.Y.: Image Books, 1979. (An insightful look at human beings that helps us to understand the general hopelessness of people and why so many grab for things like money, sex, and power indiscriminately.)

Smedes, Lewis B. *Mere Morality: What God Expects from Ordinary People*. Grand Rapids, Mich.: Eerdmans, 1983. (Since this book is an exposition of the Ten Commandments, it, of necessity, speaks to the issues of money, sex, and power.)

Part I
Money

Chapter 2 The Dark Side
of Money

The Bible tells us that the love of money is the root of all evils. If this is true, what should be our response to the dark side of money?

READINGS

OUR RESTLESS GNAWING GREED

Think of the misery that comes into our lives by our restless gnawing greed. We plunge ourselves into enormous debt and then take two and three jobs to stay afloat. We uproot our families with unnecessary moves just so we can have a more prestigious house. We grasp and grab and never have enough. And most destructive of all, our flashy cars and sports spectaculars and back-yard pools have a way of crowding out much interest in civil rights or inner city poverty or the starved masses of India.

—Richard J. Foster

THE STANDARD OF TRUE RIGHTEOUSNESS

Here I was renewedly confirmed in my mind that the Lord . . . is graciously moving in the hearts of people to draw them off from the desire of wealth and to bring them into such an humble, lowly way of living that they may see their way clearly to repair to the standard of true righteousness, and may not only break the yoke of oppression, but may know him to be their strength and support in times of outward affliction.

—John Woolman

THE EXACT OPPOSITE OF GOD'S WORK

Mammon's work is the exact opposite of God's work. Given this opposition, we understand why Jesus demands a choice between Mammon and God. He is not speaking of just any other power, just any other god; he is speaking of the one who goes directly against God's action, the one who makes "nongrace" reign in the world.

—Jacques Ellul

THE IRRATIONAL IN PEOPLE

[Money] seems to bring out the irrational in people. It taps the deepest layers of the personality and triggers emotions such as greed and envy, love and security. The desire to obtain enough money to achieve one's desired standard of living is in the realm of realistic behavior. The desire to accumulate extreme wealth is irrational. Beyond a certain point, added wealth cannot increase the opulence of one's style of living or increase one's happiness. Yet the dream of having millions is common to most Americans.

—Herb Goldberg and Robert T. Lewis

A BIBLICAL LIFESTYLE

A biblical lifestyle cannot have wealth as a goal. The biblical authors and Jesus for the most part distrust wealth. It is possessed by the powerful of this age who oppress the poor. It is gathered at the expense of the poor. . . . And wealth is highly seductive, luring its possessors into compromise with this age in order to retain (or increase) it. At best wealth is questionable, and at worst it (is)

16

both damning and damned, since it connects one to the world system which stands under God's judgment.

—Peter H. Davids

DAILY SCRIPTURE READINGS

Sunday:	The "Woes" / Luke 6:24–26
Monday:	The Rich Young Ruler / Matthew 19:16–22
Tuesday:	The Foolish Farmer / Luke 12:15–21
Wednesday:	A Startling Evangelism / Matthew 8:18–22
Thursday:	The Needle's Eye / Matthew 19:23–26
Friday:	The Treasure and the Heart / Matthew 6:19–21
Saturday:	A Den of Robbers / Mark 11:15–19

STUDY QUESTIONS

1. Why do you think money was the second most recurring theme for Jesus? (The kingdom of God was number one.)

2. Do you think I have overstated Jesus' emphasis upon the dark side of money? Understated it?

3. What are some of the ways you have seen the distortion of money as a sign of God's blessing? Why are these teachings deficient? What is the "kernel of truth" upon which they are based?

4. I write that current teachings on stewardship are a distortion because they do not reckon with money as a spiritual power. Does the teaching you have heard on stewardship bear this out? Would your tendency be to agree with what I have said here, or to dispute it?

5. Is the idea of money as a "power" new to you?

6. Do you think Jesus' radical criticism of wealth is an attempt to teach by hyperbole, or a straightforward statement of the truth?

7. Do you find it hard to admit your wealth?

8. Do you have childhood memories about money that have made a positive impact on your life? What memories have had a negative influence?

9. How did your parents influence your attitude toward money? Did they ever talk with you about money's dark side?

10. Is there anyone you can trust to guide you through the money maze?

CREATIVE SERENDIPITIES

SERENDIPITY #1

"Seek ye first the kingdom of God, and his righteousness; and all these things shall be added unto you" (Matt. 6:33, KJV).

Begin by reading Matthew 6:19–34. Then, in the privacy of your own home, write out a three-page autobiography. Divide your life into three general parts: childhood, adolescence, adulthood.

Consider the influence of money upon you as a child. What general attitude toward money did you pick up from your parents? Did you feel rich or poor? What is your happiest memory regarding money? Your saddest memory?

Consider the influence of money upon you as a teenager. What were your first money-earning experiences? How did you feel about your first major purchase—a car, for example? Was money a high priority in your adolescent years? Did you have any major embarrassments over a lack of money? Were you taught how to budget money? How to save? How to invest?

Consider the role of money in your life as an adult. Are you a "better safe than sorry" person, or a "nothing ventured, nothing gained" person? How does that affect

18

your use of money? Do you enjoy giving money away? How much of a "cushion" do you need to feel secure?

If at all possible, share your autobiography with one other person. It is best if this could be someone who has gone through the same process and will share his or her autobiography with you. If this person can be your spouse, all the better. If you have no human being with which to share, give your story up to God, for he listens with great empathy. Close your sharing with prayer.

SERENDIPITY #2

"The love of money is the root of all evils" (1 Tim. 6:10).

If at all possible, gather in a small group of not more than ten people. When you are ready to begin, have everyone sit quietly, prayerfully, while one person reads 1 Timothy 6:9–10 out loud three times, with a time of silence after each reading.

Then, without talking, place a "prayer chair" in the middle of the group, and one by one, allow each member of the group to sit in the chair while the others gather around and lovingly pray for him or her. Pray with the laying on of hands, and pray specifically for the defeat of money's dark side. It is best that the person being prayed for *not* talk, so that no person in the group feels pressured into talking about things that are better left unsaid. Pray that the spiritual power of money be made subservient to Christ, that greed be conquered, that covetousness be vanquished, that anxiety be outwitted.

It is essential that every member of the group have a turn in the prayer chair. All of us need the grace of prayer; we are not sufficient in ourselves. If emotions surface, allow them to be expressed freely. The group should continue to minister tenderly and wait patiently until any tears, or laughter, have been shared.

When prayer is completed, dismiss without further

sharing. This is one of those things that does not belong in a "testimony meeting." Jesus' instruction to tell no one applies to this kind of experience.

If you have no group with which to meet, you can go through the same experience having Jesus himself pray for you, for he is truly there with you.

Chapter 3 The Light Side of Money

Money has immense power for good. Let us consider some of the many ways it can be serviceable for Christ and his kingdom.

READINGS

MONEY AS AN INSTRUMENT OF LOVE

In the modern world there are two ways we can use our money as an instrument of love. First, the use of our money may lead us into further personal involvement in the lives of the "neighbor" in need. . . . A second way of using our money is to give it to organizations that minister to others. . . . But whether we become financially involved in immediate situations of need or whether we give to philanthropic organizations, the end result can be the same. Money, which has been so maligned as a source of evil, can also become a powerful instrument of life.

—Edward W. Bauman

POSSESSIONS . . . AS THE GIFTS OF GOD

For he who holds possessions . . . as the gifts of God; and ministers from them to the God who gives them for the salvation of men; and knows that he possesses them more for the sake of the brethren than his own; and is superior to the possession of them, not the slave of the things he possesses; . . . is able with cheerful mind to bear their removal equally with their abundance.

—Clement of Alexandria

THE STANDARD OF VALUE

In the world money is the standard of value. . . . It is, however, not only thus in the kingdom of this world, but in the kingdom of heaven, too, that a man is judged by his money, and yet on a different principle. The world asks, *what* does a man own; Christ asks, *how* does he use it? The world thinks more about the money getting; Christ, about the money giving. And when a man gives, the world still asks, *what* does he give? Christ asks, *how* does he give? The world looks at the money and its amount, Christ, at the man and his motive.

—Andrew Murray

DRY WELLS

While I am talking to the Christie family, a handsome, bearded Moslem steps out of the crowd and says something to the village chief. I am told he is the owner of one of the few wells still producing in Singhali, but it is nearly dry and must be deepened. One of the Christians tells me this man, facing disaster himself, has continued to share the water in his well with Moslem and Christian alike.

When I tell him that his well will be one of the first projects in the village with which we will help, his flow of speech stops in midsentence. He just stands with his mouth open. No words came, but his soul spoke richly through the pools which formed in his eyes. With no attempt to wipe them dry, he just stood there and sobbed. He clutched my hand and would not let go.

—Stanley Mooneyham

Money is so identified with us in our human situation that it, like ourselves, exists in two worlds, the world of sin and rebellion against God, and the world of graced obedience to God. An intrinsic part of the human situation and condition, it is an entirely paradoxical reality. Outside of God, it operates as a power antithetical to God; thus, one cannot serve God and Mammon. Subject to the reign of God, it becomes a vehicle of obedience, thanksgiving, love and joy—that which is good and supportive of human existence as a creature before the Creator. Unless this striking, powerful duality of function is recognized, we can never rightly position ourselves with respect to money.

—Robert P. Meye

DAILY SCRIPTURE READINGS

Sunday: The Experience of Abraham / Genesis 12:1–3; 13:1–2

Monday: The Experience of Job / Job 1:1–3; 42:10–17

Tuesday: The Experience of Solomon / 1 Kings 3:10–13; 10:1–7

Wednesday: Altogether Joyful / Deuteronomy 16:15; Malachi 3:10

Thursday: Wealthy Women and a Widow / Luke 8:2–3; Mark 12:41–44

Friday: Joseph and Nicodemus / Matthew 27:57–60; John 19:38–40

Saturday: Bountiful Sowing / 2 Corinthians 9:6–12

STUDY QUESTIONS

1. Do you think there is a conflict between the Old Testament and the New Testament teaching regarding money?

2. Do you think the Book of Job teaches that God rewards the righteous? Or does it teach that righteousness is a matter that is independent of wealth?

3. Could Solomon be a good example of Christian stewardship?

4. Do you think that Paul's teaching on giving in 2 Corinthians 8 and 9 (which was to encourage the church to contribute to the collection for Jerusalem Christians) has universal application, or only local application? If your answer is universal, how would you interpret in modern society his concern "that there may be equality" (2 Cor. 8:14)?

5. I write that provision is a "gracious gift of a loving God," and yet most of us have worked very hard for whatever provisions we have. Is my statement about provision as a gift just pious "gobbledygook," or is there something to it? In your own experience, do you see ways in which provision is a gift? Does such an experience enhance your relationship with God?

6. Is there any way in which the Bible's insistence upon God's absolute right to property should affect our real estate practices?

7. Switch the giving question from "How much of my money should I give to God?" to "How much of God's money should I keep to myself?" What impact does that have on the way you view giving?

8. Are there ways in which you identify with Dr. Menninger's patient who said, "I get such terror when I think of giving some of it to somebody!"? If you cannot identify at all with that statement, why do you think your reaction is so different?

9. Think of two experiences in your life in which God has used money to teach you about trust.

10. What are some specific ways individuals and churches can cultivate the spirit of thanksgiving?

CREATIVE SERENDIPITIES

SERENDIPITY #1

"The earth is the LORD's and the fullness thereof" (Ps. 24:1).

Using three-by-five cards, write out a list of five ways that money has enhanced your life or the lives of others. Use one item per card. Don't be afraid to emphasize the positive side of money. Then gather up all the cards, shuffle them, and redistribute them to group members. Have different people read what is written on their cards. Take turns. As the items are read, discuss together ways in which that particular experience could bring a person closer to God.

After everyone has shared, have someone read Psalm 24, noting especially the connection between worship and the recognition that the earth is the Lord's. Finally, read the psalm again, but this time read antiphonally, with half the group asking the questions and the other half responding.

SERENDIPITY #2

"Spend the money for whatever you desire . . . and you shall eat there before the LORD your God and rejoice, you and your household" (Deut. 14:26).

Plan a joyous holy thanksgiving party. As a preparation, read Deuteronomy 14:22–29. According to this passage, it is certainly permissible to use tithe money to finance this event, so do so with liberality. Buy what you think would make it an especially festive and celebrative experience. Make thanksgiving and praise prominent. Ban all pious speeches—they have no place at such an event—but perhaps you will want to concoct a holy shout.

25

Sing, laugh, dance, eat, and in general rejoice in God's goodness.

Chapter 4 Kingdom Use
of Unrighteous
Mammon

Jesus teaches us how to *use* mammon without *serving* it.

READINGS

HOARDING IS IDOLATRY

Earthly goods are given to be used, not to be collected. In the wilderness God gave Israel the manna every day, and they had no need to worry about food and drink. Indeed, if they kept any of the manna over until the next day, it went bad. In the same way, the disciple must receive his portion from God every day. If he stores it up as a permanent possession, he spoils not only the gift, but himself as well, for he sets his heart on his accumulated wealth, and makes it a barrier between himself and God. Where our treasure is, there is our trust, our security, our consolation and our God. Hoarding is idolatry.

—Dietrich Bonhoeffer

THE MINISTRY OF MONEY

There are those who are called to the ministry of money. The gift of giving is a vital and valid spiritual gift, and essential to it is the task of using money for the common good. Jesus told us to make "friends of the mammon of unrighteousness" (Luke 16:9, KJV); that is, make Kingdom use of material goods. It is a much needed ministry among us.

Simplicity always calls us to a simple lifestyle, but it does not always call us to a reduction in income. God calls some to increase their income in order to use it for the good of all.

—Richard J. Foster

SAVING VS. GIVING

Never let your expenses exceed your income. . . . It is impossible to lay down any general rules as to "saving all we can," and "giving all we can." In this, it seems, we must needs be directed, from time to time, by the unction of the Holy One.

—John Wesley

BUDGETING IS PLANNED SPENDING

Budgeting is planned spending! Doesn't that sound easy?

And budgeting *is* easy when you understand its purpose, follow a workable system, and use it to maximize the family income. A family that knows where its money is going can usually make it go farther.

—George Fooshee, Jr.

ONE OF THE MOST BLATANT FORMS OF MAMMONISM

The place that insurance occupies in our lives—how and why we participate in it—deserves careful evaluation in any Christian approach to contemporary economics. I want to question some of the standard assumptions. . . . It seems to me that insurance may be one of the most blatant forms of mammonism in contemporary society.

—Virgil Vogt

DAILY SCRIPTURE READINGS

Sunday: Do Not Serve Mammon / Matthew 6:24
Monday: Learn to Use Mammon / Luke 16:1–9
Tuesday: Dethrone Mammon / Acts 19:18–20
Wednesday: God's Chosen Fast / Isaiah 58:6–9
Thursday: A Matter of Equality / 2 Corinthians 8:13–15
Friday: Jubilee Generosity / Leviticus 25:8–17
Saturday: Jubilee Generosity / Luke 19:1–10

STUDY QUESTIONS

1. Read both Matthew 6:24 and Luke 16:9 and discuss the tension between these two passages. I have made one attempt at resolving the tension. What do you think?

2. Jesus said, "The sons of this world are wiser in their own generation than the sons of light." With regard to money, what are some things we might learn from "the sons of this world"?

3. Is the idea of the unrighteousness of mammon new to you? What distortions could this teaching lead to? In what ways does this teaching help us?

4. What are some ways you have found to lay up "treasures in heaven"? Are there other things you would like to do?

5. If God, rather than money, is to control decisions, how would you go about determining if you should purchase a home computer?

6. Is the idea of using money without serving money a genuine distinction, or only a difference in semantics?

7. I give seven action steps to help us master mammon. Is any one of the steps particularly helpful to you? Can you think of other steps?

8. How can you reject money's sacred character?

9. What is your response to my six affirmations on Christians in business? What would you add?

10. Do unions help, or hinder, the employer-employee relationship? Can you think of any better way to protect the interests of employees?

CREATIVE SERENDIPITIES

SERENDIPITY #1

"Make friends for yourselves by means of unrighteous mammon" (Luke 16:9).

Read out loud Jesus' parable of the unjust steward, Luke 16:1–13. As wrong as the steward's actions were, Jesus focused on the one thing he did right—he took money and used it for noneconomic purposes. Now, let us suppose your group had been given a hundred thousand dollars to use in whatever ways you felt might most advance Christ's kingdom. Brainstorm on how you might most effectively use the money. Remember, your resources, while considerable, are limited. Will you use the money to make more money so you can take on a greater project? Will you give it away, and, if so, do you give to several concerns, or only one?

If your group is large enough, form several small groups and work on this, then come together at the end of the session and share your plans with each other. Then try to evaluate which group made the wisest use of the money.

SERENDIPITY #2

"So, whether you eat or drink, or whatever you do, do all to the glory of God" (1 Cor. 10:31).

Read James 4:13–16. Consider the implications of this

passage for the business enterprise. The focus of this session is to identify with those in the world of business.

Think of the individuals in your city who own businesses or who are otherwise involved in the business world. You may want to compile a small list. Now, the task is to learn to pray with some degree of seriousness for these business people.

First, ask the Lord to help you enter into their world: to sense the stress and strain of their daily activity, to feel the constant temptation of ethical compromise, to understand the forces of competition, to feel the weight of decisions. First, pray for them as individuals with needs and hurts, hopes and aspirations. Then pray for their families. Bless the family; pray for healthy family relationships; pray for the family's protection. Finally, pray for the business decisions and daily activities of each person; for strength, wisdom, and the ability to be wise as a serpent and harmless as a dove.

Then, within the next week or so, stop by the place of business of one of the individuals for whom you prayed. Unless you are certain of its appropriateness, say nothing about the prayer experience. Simply get to know the person in the context of his or her daily work. Often they will show you around the factory or office. As you share together, inwardly be praying for the person and his or her business. The visit, no doubt, will help you know how to pray more effectively for this person who has been called to be a light in the world of business.

Chapter 5 The Vow of Simplicity

Simplicity means a life of freedom and joy.

READINGS

BE NOT ANXIOUS!

Be not anxious! Earthly possessions dazzle our eyes and delude us into thinking that they can provide security and freedom from anxiety. Yet all the time they are the very source of all anxiety. If our hearts are set on them, our reward is an anxiety whose burden is intolerable. Anxiety creates its own treasures, and they in turn beget further care. When we seek for security in possessions we are trying to drive out care with care, and the net result is the precise opposite of our anticipations. The fetters which bind us to our possessions prove to be cares themselves.

—Dietrich Bonhoeffer

SIMPLICITY IS A RIGHTNESS OF THE SOUL

Simplicity is a rightness of the soul which cuts away all useless turning back upon ourselves and upon our own behaviour. It is different from sincerity. Sincerity is a virtue below simplicity. We see lots of people who are sincere without being simple. They say nothing which they do not believe to be true. They only want to seem what they are, but they constantly fear to seem what they are not. They are always studying themselves, going over all their words and all their thoughts, and going back over all that they have done, afraid of having said or done too much. These people are sincere, but they are not simple.

—François Fénelon

TEN CONTROLLING PRINCIPLES

First, buy things for their usefulness rather than their status. . . .
Second, reject anything that is producing an addiction in you. . . .
Third, develop a habit of giving things away. . . .
Fourth, refuse to be propagandized by the custodians of modern gadgetry. . . .
Fifth, learn to enjoy things without owning them. . . .
Sixth, develop a deeper appreciation for the creation. . . .
Seventh, look with a healthy skepticism at all "buy now, pay later" schemes. . . .
Eighth, obey Jesus' instructions about plain, honest speech. . . .
Ninth, reject anything that will breed the oppression of others. . . .
Tenth, shun whatever would distract you from your main goal. . . .

—Richard J. Foster

THE BLESSEDNESS OF POSSESSING NOTHING

I have said that Abraham possessed nothing. . . . He had everything, *but he possessed nothing.* There is the spiritual secret. There is the sweet theology of the heart which can be learned only in the school of renunciation. The books on systematic theology overlook this, but the wise will understand.

—A. W. Tozer

Life on this earth is not about *consuming as much as we can afford*, but about some very simple things, which can be expressed in very simple words like:

> Do for others what you want others to do for you;
> Love your neighbor as you love yourself;
> Prove all things, hold fast that which is good.

—E. F. Schumacher

DAILY SCRIPTURE READINGS

Sunday: The Single Eye / Matthew 6:22–24
Monday: Do Not Be Anxious / Luke 12:22–34
Tuesday: Seek First His Kingdom / Matthew 6:25–33
Wednesday: Show No Partiality / James 2:1–9
Thursday: First They Gave Themselves / 2 Corinthians 8:1–7
Friday: The Gift of Giving / Romans 12:8
Saturday: Contentment / Philippians 4:10–13

STUDY QUESTIONS

1. How does the vow of simplicity differ from the monastic vow of poverty?

2. In your own words finish this sentence, "Simplicity means . . ."

3. Of the seven principles of giving, which ones are you prepared to say yes to and which ones do you have reservations about?

4. What experiences have you had in learning proportionate giving?

5. Have you felt the tension between reasoned giving and risk giving?

6. Have you seen giving used as a power play? Are there ways that could be avoided in your church?

7. Have you made out a caring will? If not, would you do so right away?

8. What have you found to be helpful in teaching your children about money? Have you found ways to help children understand the dark side of money?

9. List five inward attitudes and five outward actions that would embody the vow of simplicity in the context of your world.

10. As a disciple of Jesus Christ, are you now prepared to take a vow of simplicity?

CREATIVE SERENDIPITIES

SERENDIPITY #1

"There was not a needy person among them" (Acts 4:34).

Read Acts 4:32–37. This passage tells the story of the generous sharing and caring of the early Christian community. As far as we can tell, they were not commanded to do this by God or even told that what they were doing was right. What we see is a group of people set free by the Holy Spirit who are learning what it means to love their neighbor. Barnabas becomes a kind of paradigm for this loving, giving quality of life.

Now, what Barnabas kinds of acts can you do today? In other words, what actions would reflect the same caring spirit to your world that Barnabas's sale of his property did to his world? Perhaps you would like to jot down two or three items. If you are in a group, you might want to share your items with each other. Now, is there one of these things that you should do this week?

"Have no anxiety about anything" (Phil. 4:6).

This experience is best done in the context of a loving and like-minded fellowship, but if you are alone, do not worry; instructions for individuals will follow. Gather together those who are ready to commit themselves to a vow of simplicity. You might want to meet in your church sanctuary. For the first half hour or so, follow Paul's admonition to "sing psalms and hymns and spiritual songs with thankfulness in your hearts to God" (Col. 3:16b). Worship freely and reverently. Be baptized into a sense of the love of God. Allow whispered prayers of adoration and praise to arise as the Spirit directs.

When there is a sense of being gathered and melted into the love of God, wait together before God in silent meditation. Do not be quick to break the silence.

As each individual is ready, he or she may go to the altar and kneel; while others gather around and lay hands upon the one kneeling. Now consecrate this person to God in his or her commitment to take the vow of simplicity. Expect God's power to flow through you and into the person being consecrated for their ability to live faithfully in simplicity. Allow ample opportunity and time for every individual who wants to be so consecrated.

If you cannot find another individual to join you in this consecration service, you may do it alone. Kneel and invite the Lord Jesus Christ to consecrate you as you take up the vow of simplicity. Do not feel you are alone, for he is truly with you. Allow his word to dwell in you richly, and allow his prayer for you to have its full effect. There is no need to hurry. When you sense the prayer is completed, thank him, just thank him!

BOOKS ON MONEY

The books in this section are organized into the following categories:

The Devotional Masters
Political, Psychological, and Economic Theory
Biblical, Theological, and Ethical Studies
Simplicity and Life-Style
Money and Justice
Money Management and Other Practical Matters

THE DEVOTIONAL MASTERS

Law, William. *A Serious Call to a Devout and Holy Life—The Spirit of Love.* Edited by Paul G. Stanwood. New York: Paulist Press, 1978. (A classic work on the spiritual life. Chapter 6 particularly takes up the use of money. Described by Law himself as "the great obligations and great advantages of making a wise and religious use of our estates and fortunes.")

Perkins, William. *Treatise of Conscience.* Cambridge, 1606. *The American Experience.* No. 482. Amsterdam: Theatrvm Orbis Terrarvm Ltd., 1972. (An old work that contains wise counsel under such chapter headings as, "How Far a Man May With Good Conscience Desire and Seek Riches," "How a Man May With Good Conscience Profit and Use Riches," "Whether a Man May Voluntarily Give Away All and Live Upon Alms.")

Tozer, A. W. *The Pursuit of God.* Harrisburg, Pa.: Christian Publications, 1948. (This excellent little book contains a magnificent chapter entitled "The Blessedness of Possessing Nothing." The book is worth reading for those ten pages alone. Basically it is a discussion of Abraham and his experience of giving up Isaac, which made him "a man utterly obedient, a man who possessed nothing.")

POLITICAL, PSYCHOLOGICAL, AND ECONOMIC THEORY

Becker, Ernest. *Escape From Evil.* New York: Free Press, 1975. (This book contains an important chapter entitled "Money: The

37

New Universal Immortality Ideology" in which he attempts to help us see how we moderns have made money the new immortality, replacing the immortality ideas of the various religions.)

Bornemann, Ernest, ed. *The Psychoanalysis of Money*. New York: Urizen Books, 1976. (This book brings together some of the major works on the nature and psychology of money and provides a critical commentary upon them. It covers virtually every writer of significance in this field, from Sigmund Freud to Norman Brown. It includes a bibliography of over one hundred books of psychological writings on the theory of money. By bringing all these writings together, I think Bornemann helps us to see the ways in which money is more than just a passive material medium of exchange. Money is real power.)

Boulding, Kenneth E. *The Economy of Love and Fear*. Belmont, Calif.: Wadsworth, 1973. (A very provocative little book on a new way to look at economics, from one of the world's most highly respected economists. It is an attempt to postulate what is called "grants economics.")

Brown, Norman O. *Life Against Death: The Psychoanalytical Meaning of History*. Middletown, Conn.: Wesleyan University Press, 1959. (His chapter entitled "Filthy Lucre" is extremely important because of its attempt to pull together the basic ideas for a sacred theory of money power.)

Goldberg, Herb, and Robert T. Lewis. *Money Madness*. New York: William Morrow, 1978. (This book seeks to "unravel the psychological threads that entangle most of us in one form or another of money madness." It looks at self-destructive behavior and the various obsessions we have regarding money, such as saving money out of insecurity, feeling guilty about spending money even for necessities, using money to gain superiority, etc.)

Knight, James A. *For the Love of Money*. New York: J. B. Lippincott, 1968. (James Knight is a minister and a psychiatrist, and he brings both perspectives to bear on the subject of money. He is seeking to understand our behavior toward money, and in doing so, he looks at children, adolescents, and adults. Of particular interest is the chapter "The Anatomy of Giving.")

Menninger, Karl. *Whatever Became of Sin?* New York: Hawthorne Books, 1973. (This is an important book for many reasons, but I include it here because of the section "The Sins of Envy, Greed, Avarice, and Affluence.")

Schumacher, E. F. *The Age of Plenty: A Christian View*. Edinburgh: Saint Andrew Press, 1974. (A very meaningful little booklet by the author of *Small Is Beautiful*. He attempts to work on the question of what economics might look like if it were infused with a Christian value system.)

Smith, Adam. *An Inquiry Into the Nature and Causes of the Wealth of Nations*. New York: P. F. Collier & Son, 1937. (A book important for its influence upon American capitalism. Though it has had less impact in modern years because of the rise of Keynesian economics, it is important still in any attempt to understand the modern spirit of capitalism.)

Weber, Max. *The Protestant Ethic and the Spirit of Capitalism*. Trans. by Talcott Parsons. New York: Charles Scribner's, 1958. (An influential book. It attempts to trace the relationship between Calvinism and the rise of the spirit of capitalism.)

BIBLICAL, THEOLOGICAL, AND ETHICAL STUDIES

Bauman, Edward W. *Where Your Treasure Is*. Arlington, Va.: Bauman Bible Telecasts, 1980. (Helpful reflections on numerous aspects of money and the spiritual life.)

Beckmann, David M. *Where Faith and Economics Meet: A Christian Critique*. Minneapolis: Augsburg, 1981. (A good discussion of the consumer mentality by someone who is a Christian pastor and a World Bank economist.)

Carlson, Martin E. *Why People Give*. New York: National Council of Churches Press for Stewardship and Benevolence, 1968. (This study of giving tries to bring together insights from motivational psychology and Christian ethics. The author is seeking to determine when giving can be considered Christian and when it cannot.)

Ellul, Jacques. *Money & Power*. Trans. by LaVonne Neff. Downers Grove, Ill.: Inter-Varsity Press, 1984. (This book really deals with the money question; the issue of power is wholly secondary. Written some years ago but only recently translated into English. When Ellul writes people need to listen!)

Hengel, Martin. *Property and Riches in the Early Church*. Philadelphia: Fortress Press, 1974. (A scholarly study of the Christian approach to property and riches from the time of Christ—with a brief discussion of Old Testament views—to about the fourth century. Extensive attention is given to the ante-Nicene Fathers.)

Hollis, Allen. *The Bible and Money*. New York: Hawthorn Books, 1976.

(Allen Hollis attempts in this book to forge a theology of money. His main burden is to help us know what the Bible actually says about money; hence, there are chapters on what Leviticus, Deuteronomy, and Kings teach about money, what Psalms and Proverbs teach about money, what Jesus teaches about money, and what other New Testament writers teach about money. He then draws four major biblical themes from his study: the need for control of human instincts with respect to money, money's fragility, money's corrupting nature, and money's positive nature.)

Mullin, Redmond. *The Wealth of Christians.* Exeter: Paternoster Press, 1983. (A thoughtful book on the many sources for the current Christian attitude toward money. It looks at a considerable array of practical issues, such as marketing, philanthropy, charitable organizations, fund raising, etc. and concludes with numerous proposals.)

Piper, Otto A. *The Christian Meaning of Money.* Englewood Cliffs, N.J.: Prentice-Hall, 1965. (In this book, Otto Piper attempts to help us think theologically and ethically about money. He examines the nature of money in the context of ethical considerations, looks at biblical perspectives, and considers the role of money in personal and public life.)

Taylor, Richard K. *Economics and the Gospel.* Philadelphia: United Church Press, 1973. (A powerful analysis of economic justice in the context of Christian ethics.)

Vogt, Virgil. *Treasure in Heaven: The Biblical Teaching about Money, Finances, and Possessions.* Ann Arbor, Mich.: Servant Books, 1982. (A very meaningful and readable study written by the leader of Reba Place Fellowship, a Christian community in Evanston, Illinois.)

SIMPLICITY AND LIFE-STYLE

Cooper, John C. *Finding a Simpler Life.* Philadelphia: United Church Press, 1974. (Lays the groundwork for an authentic vision of simplicity in modern society.)

Eller, Vernard. *The Simple Life.* Grand Rapids, Mich.: Eerdmans, 1973. (A look at inward simplicity through the eyes of the Gospel records and the writings of Søren Kierkegaard.)

Fager, Charles E. "The Quaker Testimony of Simplicity." *Quaker Religious Thought* (Summer 1972), pp. 2–30. (Helps us to wrestle with Christian simplicity by looking at one group that has given considerable thought to this question.)

Foster, Richard J. *Freedom of Simplicity*. San Francisco: Harper & Row, 1981. (Attempts to place simplicity within the context of the whole of Christian devotion and to bring together the various emphases upon inner and outer simplicity.)

Gish, Arthur G. *Beyond the Rat Race*. Scottdale, Penn.: Herald Press, 1973. (Gish launches an uncompromising attack on materialism and a vigorous call to outward simplicity that is guaranteed to disturb you to the core.)

O'Connor, Elizabeth. *Letters to Scattered Pilgrims*. San Francisco: Harper & Row, 1979. (As in her earlier writings, *Call to Commitment* and *Journey Inward, Journey Outward*, Elizabeth O'Connor continues in this book to chronicle the experiences and insights of the Church of the Savior in Washington, D.C. It contains two excellent chapters on money and describes their process of writing a money autobiography.)

Sider, Ronald J. *Rich Christians in an Age of Hunger: A Biblical Study*. Downers Grove, Ill.: Inter-Varsity Press, 1977. (Extremely valuable, biblical, and practical study of the question of justice in modern society. Must reading.)

———, ed. *Living More Simply: Biblical Principles & Practical Models*. Downers Grove, Ill.: Inter-Varsity Press, 1980. (A collection of papers given at the U.S. Consultation on Simple Lifestyle. Helpful and thoughtful.)

VandenBroeck, Goldian, ed. *Less Is More: The Art of Voluntary Poverty*. New York: Harper & Row, 1978. (A compilation of helpful quotations on the money question from Christians and non-Christians alike throughout the centuries.)

Ziegler, Edward K. *Simple Living*. Elgin, Ill.: Brethren Press, 1974. (A look at simplicity from the perspective of the Church of the Brethren.)

MONEY AND JUSTICE

Galilea, Segundo. *Following Jesus*. Trans. by Helen Phillips. Maryknoll, N.Y.: Orbis Books, 1981. (A helpful discussion of Christian discipleship from a South American perspective. Includes a meaningful chapter entitled "Following Jesus in the Poor.")

Mooneyham, W. Stanley. *What Do You Say to a Hungry World?* Waco, Tex.: Word Books, 1975. (Written by the former president of World Vision International, this is a genuinely helpful book in sensitizing us to the human tragedy of poverty. It combines both significant information about Third World needs and touching human drama. Highly recommended.)

Sider, Ronald J., ed. *Cry Justice: The Bible on Hunger and Poverty.* New York: Paulist Press; Downers Grove, Ill.: Inter-Varsity Press, 1980. (A gathering of biblical passages topically around the themes of justice, hunger, and poverty.)

Simon, Arthur. *Bread for the World.* New York: Paulist Press; Grand Rapids, Mich.: Eerdmans, 1975. (A tremendously helpful and practical discussion of world hunger by the executive director of Bread for the World.)

MONEY MANAGEMENT AND OTHER PRACTICAL MATTERS

Fooshee, George, and Marjean Fooshee. *You Can Beat the Money Squeeze.* Old Tappan, N.J.: Fleming H. Revell, 1980; and Fooshee, George, Jr. *You Can Be Financially Free.* Old Tappan, N.J.: Fleming H. Revell, 1976. (Two books that are intently practical. Since the author is the president of a bill-collecting agency, he sees on a daily basis the trap people put themselves into by overspending. He packs in a lot of really sane counsel on a whole range of money management issues: budgeting, revolving charge accounts, savings, installment buying, taxes, wills, mortgages, and more.)

Loeb, Marshall. *Marshall Loeb's Money Guide.* Boston: Little, Brown, 1983. (A strictly common sense how-to book by the managing editor of *Money* magazine. It covers a great variety of topics, from annuities to wills.)

VanCaspel, Venita. *The Power of Money Dynamics.* Reston, Va.: Reston Publishing, 1983. (This is the standard in the field of financial management. Venita VanCaspel has also written three other best-selling books on financial matters, *Money Dynamics, The New Money Dynamics,* and *Money Dynamics for the 1980s. The Power of Money Dynamics* covers a very large range of subjects: the stock market, real estate, tax liabilities and assets, life insurance, retirement, and much more. If one feels called into seriously dealing with money, this is an essential book on learning to be wise as a serpent.)

Weinstein, Grace W. *Children & Money.* New York: Charterhouse, 1975. (A sensible guide for parents in helping children learn to deal responsibly with money. It covers a host of practical considerations, such as allowances, pay and family chores, checking accounts, teenagers and charge cards, and more. The author also has a little Public Affairs Pamphlet [No. 593] entitled *Teaching Children About Money,* which covers the same ground in a brief format.)

——. *The Lifetime Book of Money Management.* New York: NAL Books, 1983. (A comprehensive book on money management. It covers nearly every conceivable subject: budgets, checking accounts, savings accounts, investment strategy, tax shelters, buying a house or automobile, life and health insurance, estate planning, and more. It is the only book I found that has an entire chapter on financing your children's college education. Very well done throughout.)

Part II
Sex

Chapter 6 Sexuality and Spirituality

We are sexual beings and our sexuality does affect our spiritual well-being.

READINGS

THE GOODNESS OF SEXUAL PLEASURE

The old Christian teachers said that if man had never fallen, sexual pleasure, instead of being less than it is now, would actually have been greater. . . . Christianity has glorified marriage more than any other religion: and nearly all the greatest love poetry in the world has been produced by Christians. If anyone says that sex, in itself, is bad, Christianity contradicts him at once.

—C. S. Lewis

THREE NORMATIVE PATTERNS

I think we can locate three normative patterns for our sexual lives: . . .

1. The sexuality of every person is meant to be woven into the whole character of that person and integrated into his quest for human values.

2. The sexuality of every person is meant to be an urge toward and a means of expressing a deep personal relationship with another person.

3. The sexuality of every person is meant to move him toward a heterosexual union of committed love.

—Lewis B. Smedes

PAUL'S GREAT CONTRIBUTION

Undoubtedly, Paul's great positive contribution to Christian sexual theology lies in the manner in which he elevates the sexual union in marriage as a parable of the "great mystery" which symbolizes the union of Christ and the church. This involves a remarkable psychological understanding of intercourse as an act which is not simply a pleasurable genital function but rather one which can engage the whole person in ways which express a unique mode of commitment and self-disclosure.

—James B. Nelson

A CONTEMPORARY FALLACY

I want to end by warning you against what is a fairly widespread contemporary fallacy. . . . Today many agencies, advertising and vulgarized psychology to mention only two, try to persuade us that the flesh can be made Word, that we can come into our human inheritance by the ruthless pursuit of physical pleasure. But the flesh can never be made Word. To act and live as though it could is to condemn yourself to the torture of self-contradiction, which is hell. The flesh can never be made Word, but the Word is for ever being made flesh, and to know that is to find your true self. It is to be chaste.

—H. A. Williams

ONE FLESH

Although the union in "one flesh" is a physical union established by sexual intercourse (the conjunction of the sexual organs) it involves at the same time the whole being, and affects the personality at the deepest level. It is a union of the entire man and the entire woman.

—Derrick Sherwin Bailey

DAILY SCRIPTURE READINGS

Sunday: Male and Female / Genesis 1:26–27
Monday: Naked and Not Ashamed / Genesis 2:20–25
Tuesday: The "Knowledge" of Coitus / Genesis 4:1; 4:17; 4:25
Wednesday: Celebrating the Kiss / Song of Solomon 1:2–4
Thursday: Celebrating Beauty / Song of Solomon 7:1–9
Friday: Love's Loyalty / Song of Solomon 8:6–7
Saturday: Sexuality's Distortion / Romans 1:24–32

STUDY QUESTIONS

1. In what ways do you think our creation as male and female is related to our creation in the image of God? What implication does your answer have for the unisex movement?

2. Is it possible today to be "naked and not ashamed"?

3. Karl Barth spoke of the vacillation between "evil eroticism" and "an evil absence of eroticism." Share examples of both evils and discuss how the Church can guard against them.

4. Given its very explicit sexuality, do you feel the Song of Solomon should have been omitted from our Bible? Be able to defend your answer.

5. In Matthew 5:28 Jesus spoke of looking at a woman "lustfully." How would you define "lust"?

6. How do you interpret Jesus' statements about plucking

49

out offending eyes and cutting off offending hands (Matt. 5:29–30)?

7. How can two people become "one flesh" without destroying their individuality?

8. What reasons would you give to account for the failure in Church history to remain faithful to the Bible's positive approach to sexuality?

9. If you are in a group, discuss the thorny issue of pornography. What is it? Is it strictly a personal matter? Should there be social regulation of it?

10. Below are listed several passages that are usually thought to deal with homosexuality. Read the passages, and then try to answer the questions that follow.

   Leviticus 18:23; 20:13
   Romans 1:26–27
   1 Corinthians 6:9–10
   1 Timothy 1:9–10

a. By comparing translations or using other study helps see if you can determine if these passages do indeed deal with homosexuality.

b. Are these teachings universal—for all people at all times— or are they local and temporary?

c. Is it possible that they are dealing only with homosexuality in the promiscuous sense and not talking at all about the homosexuality that emphasizes permanent commitment?

d. Do modern scientific studies on homosexuality give us any help on thinking through these passages?

CREATIVE SERENDIPITIES

SERENDIPITY #1

"And the man and his wife were both naked, and were not ashamed" (Gen. 2:25).

Begin with silent prayer. Center on allowing God to teach you about the goodness of your body. Share together in the following litany.

Leader: We thank you, O Lord, Creator of all things,
                that your creation is good in every way.
                Thank you for creating our bodies;
                Thank you that our bodies are good
                Thank you for creating sex;
                Thank you that sex is good.
People: We thank you, Lord, for our sexuality.
Leader: We praise you, O Lord, for intimacy;
                for the fun of holding hands,
                for the thrill of kisses and caresses,
                for the playfulness of lovers,
                for the warmth of sexual intimacy.
People: We praise you, O Lord, for our sexuality.
Leader: Forgive us, O Lord, forgive us;
                for despising your good creation,
                for being ashamed of passion,
                for failing to cherish our bodies,
                for building a wall between the sexual
                and the spiritual.
People: Do forgive us, Lord. Heal us so that we can dance
                and sing and frolic in your love. Amen.

SERENDIPITY #2

"Purge me with hyssop, and I shall be clean; wash me and I shall be whiter than snow" (Ps. 51:7).

Devote this session to meditating upon the various distortions of human sexuality. With each, begin by inviting God to help you see how he intended sexuality to be in its purity, and then slowly watch its perversion. Notice what a beautiful thing it was in the beginning and what a grotesque thing it becomes.

Be especially sensitive to God's own hurt and brokenness over sexuality's distortion. Perhaps you will be allowed to enter into some of his great pain.

Finally, pray for the healing of human sexuality. Pray for people and institutions and whole cultures to be drawn out of sexuality's distortions and into sexuality's wholeness.

Chapter 7 Sexuality and Singleness

The Church can make an enormous contribution by helping singles grapple with their sexuality with honesty and integrity.

READINGS

THE DEEPEST UNITY OF HEART AND SOUL

It is possible for everyone to find the deepest unity of heart and soul without marriage. . . . There is a calling in the Church besides marriage. To remain single can lead to a very high calling if one is able to accept it deeply in one's heart. Those who give up everything, also the great gift of marriage, for Jesus, are given a great promise. Jesus is especially close to them and will be very near them at His coming.

—Heini Arnold

GOD'S HELP

We may, indeed, be sure that perfect chastity—like perfect charity—will not be attained by any merely human efforts. You must ask for God's help. Even when you have done so, it may seem to you for a long time that no help, or less help than you need, is being given. Never mind. After each failure, ask forgiveness, pick yourself up, and try again. Very often what God first helps us towards is not the virtue itself but just this power of always trying again.

—C. S. Lewis

A HOLY EMPTINESS

Celibates live out the holy emptiness in their lives by not marrying, by not trying to build for themselves a house or a fortune, by not trying to wield as much influence as possible, and by not filling their lives with events, people, or creations for which they will be remembered. They hope that by their empty lives God will be recognized as the source of all human thoughts and actions. Especially by not marrying and by abstaining from the most intimate expression of human love, the celibate becomes a living sign of the limits of interpersonal relationships and of the centrality of the inner sanctum that no human being may violate.

—Henri J. M. Nouwen

PRIZING PURITY

In forfeiting the sanctity of sex by casual, nondiscriminatory "making out" and "sleeping around," we forfeit something we cannot well do without. There is dullness, monotony, sheer boredom in all of life when virginity and purity are no longer protected and prized. By trying to grab fulfillment everywhere, we find it nowhere.

—Elisabeth Elliot

LONGING FOR INTIMACY

Single persons are often longing for the intimacy, special times, and pleasant memories of activities traditionally associated with, and limited to, romance in the conventional sense. Why not broaden our ideas so that they are not so bound up with obsessive longings for sexual expression, causing us to feel deprived without

54

that expression? We can have good companionship and pleasant times and wonderful emotional intimacy without being bound to the traditional all-or-nothing romantic love script.

—Letha Dawson Scanzoni

DAILY SCRIPTURE READINGS

Sunday: Love's Patience / Song of Solomon 2:7; 3:5; 8:4
Monday: Love's Restraint / Song of Solomon 8:8–10
Tuesday: Dealing with Lust / Matthew 5:27–28
Wednesday: Jesus' Statement on the Single Life / Matthew 19:12
Thursday: Paul's Statement on the Single Life / 1 Corinthians 7:8–9, 25–28, 32–35
Friday: Celebrating the Good and the Beautiful / Philippians 4:8
Saturday: Nurturing Nongenital Sexuality / Ephesians 4:31–32

STUDY QUESTIONS

1. Can you suggest ways for singles to express their sexuality in addition to those I have listed?

2. Am I right when I say rather bluntly that "biblical teaching places a clear veto on sexual intercourse for single people"? If I am right, do you think the Bible is right in doing so?

3. There is a specifically Christian reason for reserving coitus for marriage that goes beyond the normal concerns of pregnancy, venereal disease, etc. What is it?

4. Can sexual fantasies ever be positive in nature? If so, how do you distinguish them from destructive sexual fantasies?

5. What reason would you give for why the Bible does not discuss masturbation?

6. What attitude do *you* think Christians should have toward masturbation? Why?

7. Do you think it would be wise for the Church to establish specific guidelines for the practice of "passion under control"?

8. Do you think people can have experiences of "petting" that are not intended to result in genital sex?

9. Do you know of anyone who you think has a call of God to a single life? Does the idea make you feel uneasy?

10. What can the Church do for single people who feel no call to singleness and truly wish to be married?

CREATIVE SERENDIPITIES

SERENDIPITY #1

"I say to you that every one who looks at a woman lustfully has already committed adultery with her in his heart" (Matt. 5:28).

The matter of sexual fantasy is not an easy topic to discuss, so be sensitive to each other's need to refrain from sharing. Perhaps it would be helpful to begin by discussing when you think looking or fantasizing turns into lust. Can you develop any guidelines? Next, have those that would like to tell of ways that sexual fantasies have been a blessing and/or a curse in their lives. What has been helpful for you in dealing with this area of life? Remember, married people are not exempt from having difficulties in this area. In fact, often married people have more difficulty dealing with this than do single people.

Allow the flow of the group to determine what should happen next. Praise. Confession, prayer, thanksgiving.

" 'All things are lawful,' but not all things are helpful. 'All things are lawful,' but not all things build up. Let no one seek his own good, but the good of his neighbor" (1 Cor. 10:23–24).

In this serendipity, we want to consider a Christian stance toward the rituals of acquaintanceship and courtship. Discuss the diagram I gave on page 129 of *Money, Sex & Power*.

How can we help each other keep commitment and intimacy in balance? Are there definite stages of commitment prior to engagement? Can you parallel stages of commitment with stages of intimacy? Or is that approach too rigid and idealistic to be helpful to people in love? Are there other ways to help each other experience the wholesome aspects of mutual affection while minimizing the dangers?

Chapter 8 Sexuality and Marriage

Marriage ushers us into the strange and awesome mystery of "one flesh" in all of its pristine fullness.

READINGS

AH, DEAR LORD

Ah, dear Lord, marriage is not an affair of nature, but a gift of God. It is the sweetest and dearest, yes, purest life. . . . How eagerly I longed for my dear ones as I lay deadly ill at Schmalkalden! . . . Now that I am by God's grace well again, I cherish my wife and children so much the more. No one is so spiritual as not to feel such inborn love and longing. For the union and communion of man and wife are a great thing.

—Martin Luther

PLAY AND LAUGHTER

We must not be totally serious about Venus.* Indeed we can't be totally serious without doing violence to our humanity. It is not for nothing that every language and literature in the world is full of jokes about sex. Many of them may be dull or disgusting and nearly all of them are old. But we must insist that they embody an attitude to Venus which in the long run endangers the Christian life far less than a reverential gravity. We must not at-

---

* The goddess of love.

tempt to find an absolute in the flesh. Banish play and laughter from the bed of love and you may let in a false goddess.

—C. S. Lewis

CHRIST IS THE LORD EVEN OF MARRIAGE

Jesus does not depreciate the body and its natural instincts, but he does condemn the unbelief which is so often latent in its desires. So far then from abolishing marriage, he sets it on a firmer basis and sanctifies it through faith. The disciple's exclusive adherence to Christ therefore extends even to his married life. Christian marriage is marked by discipline and self-denial. Christ is the Lord even of marriage.

—Dietrich Bonhoeffer

FORGIVING LOVE

When I am forgiven by my mate, I feel truly sorry for what I have done, and genuinely grateful that he nevertheless loves me and cares for me. Repentance and gratitude make me vow to try never to hurt him again. It is the forgiveness and grace which we know in love that makes us say, "I'm sorry; I'll try not to do that again." Then the relationship is renewed and the trespass is forgotten. We have the chance to begin again in a deepened and more intimate relationship, which has been strengthened because it has conquered conflict by the power of forgiving love.

—Elizabeth Achtemeier

THE DIVINE TENDERNESS OF THE SEXUAL SPHERE

Let us look at the divine tenderness of the sexual sphere. It was created for love. . . . When two people become completely one in spirit, body, and soul *with God* and *in God*, the sexual sphere is of an extremely tender and mysterious nature, uniting in the most intimate and inexpressible way. It glorifies God. . . . This marriage reflects something of the image of God.

—Heini Arnold

DAILY SCRIPTURE READINGS

Sunday: Love's Passion / Song of Solomon 3:1–4
Monday: The Wedding Night / Song of Solomon 4:12–5:1
Tuesday: Conjugal Rights / 1 Corinthians 7:3–5
Wednesday: Celebrating Marriage / John 2:1–11
Thursday: Unbelieving Mates / 1 Corinthians 7:12–16
Friday: Rules for the Christian Household / Ephesians 5:21–6:9; Colossianis 3:18–4:1
Saturday: Moses' Certificate of Divorce / Deuteronomy 24:1–4; Matthew 19:7–9

STUDY QUESTIONS

1. Explain my basis for marriage that conforms to the way of Christ. Do you agree, or disagree? Can you think of any scriptural passages that would tend to support this position? Any that would contradict it?

2. Why is it important to think of marriage as a covenant?

3. How important is romantic love to a marriage? If you are married—how important has it been in your marriage?

4. Is there any sexual activity in marriage that you feel is clearly *not* appropriate for Christians? Why?

5. What pluses or minuses do you see in the many manuals on sexual technique?

6. Can divorce ever be an act of obedience to Christ and the refusal to get a divorce be an act of disobedience?

7. What cultural situation was Jesus dealing with in his teaching on divorce?

8. What situations do *you* think justify divorce (if any)? What biblical passage or principle could you use to support your position?

9. If a divorce occurred before conversion to Christ, does that automatically mean that remarriage is acceptable?

10. How do *you* interpret Jesus' statement that "whoever marries a divorced woman commits adultery" (Matt. 5:32)?

CREATIVE SERENDIPITIES

SERENDIPITY #1

"On the third day there was a marriage at Cana in Galilee, and the mother of Jesus was there; Jesus also was invited to the marriage, with his disciples" (John. 2:1–2).

Begin by having every couple in the group tell how they met, what attracted them to each other, when they knew they were in love, and so on. Take ample time to enjoy fully the unique experience of each couple.

Next, have the other members of the group share one or two things about each couple that they especially appreciate. Every couple develops a unique personality, and this is a time to affirm those lovely, creative things that God has built into their relationship. Close by giving special prayer for each marriage. Bless the marriage in the name of the Lord. Pray healing prayers for those that are hurting. Pray protection prayers for those who are doing quite well, that their marriage will continue to prosper.

SERENDIPITY #2

"Weep with those who weep" (Romans 12:15).

This little experience is designed to center on those

who have known hurt in their marriage, especially those who have suffered the rupture of a marriage relationship. There is to be no spirit of condemnation or judgment allowed. This is a time for the healing of human hurts.

If there are people in the group who would like healing prayer, they can have others gathered around them and gently lift them into the love and care of the Father. The key here is not many words or loud words but loving words. The person being prayed for should not share anything at all. The group does not need to know who did what or why or who was at fault. They should center all their energies on the fact that there is someone in their midst who is hurting and needs love and prayer.

If there is time and energy, you might like lovingly to intercede for others that come to mind. I would suggest that it be done in the following way. Sit together quietly, and as a name comes to mind speak it out loud. Then the group prays in silence for this one, surrounding him or her with God's love and care. No word is spoken except the name of the person. This helps to discipline the group against gossip and prying into details best left unmentioned.

Chapter 9 The Vow of Fidelity

Fidelity means to affirm God's design for our sexuality in all its beauty and complexity.

READINGS

THE CHRISTIAN IS CHASTE

The Christian is chaste: he devotes his body exclusively to the service of the Body of Christ. . . . Our fellowship and communion with the crucified and glorified Body of Christ liberates us from unchastity in our own physical life. In that communion our wild physical passions are daily done to death. The Christian practises chastity and self-control, using his body exclusively in the service of building up the Body of Christ, the Church. He does the same in marriage, and thus makes it also a part of the Body of Christ.

—Dietrich Bonhoeffer

THE PROMISE TO BE TRUE

The promise, made when I am in love and because I am in love, to be true to the beloved as long as I live, commits one to being true even if I cease to be in love. A promise must be about things that I can do, about actions: no one can promise to go on feeling in a certain way. He might as well promise never to have a headache or always to feel hungry.

—C. S. Lewis

TOTAL DISARMAMENT

Finally and most importantly, love asks for a total *disarmament*. . . . When the soldier sits down to eat he lays down his weapons, because eating means peace and rest. When he stretches out his body to sleep he is more vulnerable than ever. Table and bed are the two places of intimacy where love can manifest itself in weakness. In love men and women take off all the forms of power, embracing each other in total disarmament. The nakedness of their body is only a symbol of total vulnerability and availability.

—Henri J. M. Nouwen

A FIDELITY OF SHARING

For us fidelity has much broader connotations than absolute sexual loyalty. In the best relationships there will be a fidelity of sharing. We pledge ourselves to travel the inner roads together. We will take off our masks, come out from behind our facades. We will be honest with each other.

—Charlie and Martha Shedd

THE MATURING OF LOVE

True love involves responsibility—the one for the other and both before God. . . . Only in marriage can love really unfold and mature, because only there can it find permanence and faithfulness. True love never can and never will end. That's why you should use the great words, "I love you" very sparingly.

—Walter Trobisch

DAILY SCRIPTURE READINGS

Sunday: The Paradigm of Agape / 1 Corinthians 13

Monday:	God's Original Intent / Matthew 19:1–6; Mark 10:2–12
Tuesday:	One Flesh / 1 Corinthians 6:15–20
Wednesday:	The Covenant of Fidelity / Malachi 2:13–16
Thursday:	The Mystery of Christ and the Church / Ephesians 5:28–33
Friday:	David's Infidelity / 2 Samuel 11:2–12:15
Saturday:	David's Confession / Psalm 51

STUDY QUESTIONS

1. At the beginning of this chapter, I give a little litany of seven affirmations on the meaning of fidelity. Read the seven statements to the group and discuss them among yourselves.

2. The idea of loyalty to a "calling," and in particular the "calling" of marriage, was tremendously important to the Puritans and other Christian groups. Why do contemporary Christians find it hard to relate to this idea? Do you think most Christians feel called into their marriage?

3. Why do so many couples find it hard to pray with each other?

4. Can single people really have a sense of wholeness in their sexuality without genital sex?

5. Do you think the yearning for intimacy is inherent in our creation in the image of God?

6. Can you think of any biblical evidence to support polygamy? Monogamy?

7. Do you think it is fair to ask young people who are still seeking to discover who they really are to make a lifetime commitment to marriage?

8. Is it really possible to bring a serious marital crisis to the church fellowship for discernment and guidance?

9. What do you think the Bible teaches regarding authority and submission in the Christian household?

10. What practical things could your church do for the sexually disenfranchised?

CREATIVE SERENDIPITIES

SERENDIPITY #1

"Love never ends" (1 Cor. 13:8).

Begin the meeting by having someone read 1 Corinthians 13 slowly and thoughtfully. Give opportunity for the group to meditate on the attributes of love.

Next, take every single person and every married couple in the group and, as a community, wrap your arms around them and give to them the blessing of Christ's peace. You may want to give them the gift of one of the characteristics of agape, for example, "Nancy, I'd like to give you a special increase of love's patience; Mike and Joann, we want to give you new strength to be able to endure all things." Close by singing "Amazing Grace."

SERENDIPITY #2

"Let us consider how to stir up one another to love and good works" (Heb. 10:24).

As a group, brainstorm on ways the Church can help people live the vow of fidelity, and write these on a large sheet of butcher paper. Are there some special training programs for singles that are needed? Are there ways Church life should be restructured to enhance family solidarity? What can be done to respond to the needs of the sexually disenfranchised? What resources might help—books, films, tapes, "recovery of hope" programs, and so on?

Throw ideas out as fast as possible without any evaluation whatever about their feasibility or even desirability. After plenty of ideas are listed, go back and see if there are any two or three items that the group feels particularly concerned about. Do not make a quick decision, but hold open the possibility that one or more of the items listed is a work for you to do.

BOOKS ON SEX

The books in this section are organized into the following categories:

Theology and Sexuality

Sexuality and Purity

Contemporary Issues in Sexuality

Homosexuality

Divorce and Remarriage

The Single Life

Marriage

THEOLOGY AND SEXUALITY

Bailey, Derrick Sherwin. *The Mystery of Love and Marriage: A Study of the Theology of Sexual Relation.* New York: Harper & Brothers, 1952. (This is perhaps the single most important book on the theology of "one flesh." Bailey has sought to relate "one flesh" to such important issues as sexual intercourse, divorce, the resurrection of the dead, second marriage, and more. It is both scholarly and readable—a welcome combination. You should also be aware of another book by Bailey, *Common Sense About Sexual Ethics*, [Macmillan, 1962].)

Barth, Karl. *Church Dogmatics: A Selection.* New York: Harper & Row, 1961. (For many readers, Barth's *Dogmatics* is overwhelming. This book of selected passages from the *Dogmatics* can provide you with a good entry point into the writings of this important theologian. I list the book here because of the chapters "Agape and Eros" and "Man and Woman;" they give the basis for his ethical thinking on the questions of marriage and sexual life.)

Derrick, Christopher. *Sex and Sacredness.* San Francisco: Ignatius Press, 1982. (An unapologetically Catholic effort to bring together the worlds of spirituality and sexuality. The author writes: "The Catholic Faith is an incarnational, even a carnal thing: I have heard it described as the sexiest of all the great religions" [p. 73]. It would be of interest mainly to those concerned with particular Catholic issues.)

Donnelly, Dody H. *Radical Love: An Approach to Sexual Spirituality.* Minneapolis: Winston Press, 1984. (The great burden of this book is to interpret the themes of the radical feminist movement in the language of spirituality. It represents a trend bringing spirituality and sexuality together, but seldom is the synthesis rooted in biblical revelation.)

Gundry, Patricia. *Woman Be Free!* Grand Rapids, Mich.: Zondervan, 1977. (A refreshing little book that pleas for full humanity for woman. It does some good work with the biblical material.)

Hollis, Harry, Jr. *Thank God for Sex: A Christian Model for Sexual Understanding and Behavior.* Nashville: Broadman Press, 1975. (A very readable Christian celebration of sex. It takes the context of contemporary society, the role of the Church, and the insights of theology seriously, which has resulted in a well-done book for ordinary readers.)

Jewett, Paul K. *Man as Male and Female.* Grand Rapids, Mich.: Eerdmans, 1975. (A serious theology of sexuality. Following Barth, Jewett grounds human sexuality in the *Imago Dei.* Also, he provides a rigorous examination of the New Testament texts upon which a hierarchical view of the man-woman relationship is usually based.)

Lewis, C. S. *The Four Loves.* New York: Harcourt Brace Jovanovich, 1960. (Lewis is perhaps the greatest Christian author of the twentieth century, and we can be thankful that he turned his skillful attention in this book to the question of love. He examines the four classic expressions of love—*storge* [affection], *philia* [friendship], *eros* [romantic love], and *agape* [charity].)

Nelson, James B. *Embodiment: An Approach to Sexuality and Christian Theology.* Minneapolis: Augsburg, 1978. (This book is a serious attempt to forge a Christian "sexual theology." Beginning from an incarnational premise, the author seeks to help us see what it means to be *both* sexual and spiritual. Most will find this book too heavy in its subject matter and too radical in its conclusions, but it is, nonetheless, an important and thoughtful study.)

Nouwen, Henri J. M. *Intimacy: Essays in Pastoral Psychology*. San Francisco: Harper & Row, 1969. (This slender book contains a very moving chapter under the title "Intimacy and Sexuality." In it, Nouwen helps us to understand the interconnectedness of the power question and the sex question and points the way to the possibility of love. Most helpful.)

Piper, Otto A. *The Biblical View of Sex and Marriage*. New York: Scribner's, 1960. (This is certainly among the most significant books on the Christian perspective on sex and marriage. Although written in 1960, it still contains much that is worth reading.)

————. *The Christian Interpretation of Sex*. New York: Scribner's, 1941. (One of the very early attempts to treat the matter of sexuality from a serious biblical perspective. This book is dealing, not with how we integrate our sexuality into our personalities, but rather with the divine purpose manifesting itself in sex.)

Sapp, Stephen. *Sexuality, the Bible, and Science*. Philadelphia: Fortress Press, 1977. (Sapp seeks to bring together a Christian theology of sex and current insights of the biological and social sciences. He finds no discontinuity between mind and matter, between body and spirit.)

Small, Dwight Hervery. *Christian: Celebrate Your Sexuality*. Old Tappen, N.J.: Fleming H. Revell, 1974. (A quite serious and readable book on the theology of sexuality. In this book Small is able to bring to us some of the best insights of such theologians as Karl Barth, Emil Brunner, Helmut Thielicke, and Dietrich Bonhoeffer.)

Smedes, Lewis B. *Sex for Christians*. Grand Rapids, Mich.: Eerdmans, 1976. (Smedes is always good, but here he has outdone himself. It is the best single book I know of to help Christians think through their sexuality. Must reading.)

Thielicke, Helmut. *The Ethics of Sex*. Trans. by John W. Doberstein. New York: Harper & Row, 1964. (Masterful as only Thielicke can be; obtuse as only German theologians can be. He covers just about everything, including such ancient issues as polygamy and such modern issues as artificial insemination. This book is filled with careful and valuable thought that is well worth the arduous effort of working through it.)

Trible, Phyllis. *God and the Rhetoric of Sexuality*. Philadelphia: Fortress

69

Press, 1978. (A rather scholarly biblical theology of sexuality with a special concentration upon the early chapters of Genesis, the Song of Songs, and the Book of Ruth. By carefully exegeting the Hebrew Scriptures, the author gives helpful insights into the female imagery for God.)

SEXUALITY AND PURITY

Elliot, Elisabeth. *Passion and Purity.* Old Tappan, N.J.: Fleming H. Revell, 1984. (Written by the author of *Through Gates of Splendor* and *Shadow of the Almighty,* this is a clear call to singles to bring their sexual passions under spiritual discipline. She uses the tender love story of her courtship with Jim Elliot as a backdrop for the book.)

Lutzer, Erwin W. *Living with Your Passions: A Christian's Guide to Sexual Purity.* Wheaton, Ill.: Victor Books, 1983. (A simple little book on dealing with sexual desires. He covers such topics as sexual fantasies, adultery, lust, homosexuality, and masturbation. The counsels for redirecting behavior often fail to recognize the complexity of the situation, but if this is recognized, the book can serve as a helpful encouragement for sexual purity.)

Trobisch, Walter, comp. *I Loved a Girl: A Private Correspondence Between Two Young Africans and Their Pastor.* New York: Harper & Row, 1965. (A series of letters between young Africans and their pastor that contains helpful counsel.)

White, John. *Eros Defiled.* Downers Grove, Ill.: Inter-Varsity Press, 1977. (Dr. White is a psychiatrist who, through his writings, has helped the Christian world interface psychiatry and Christianity. This book is a compassionate look at deviant sexual behavior.)

White, Mel. *Lust: The Other Side of Love.* Old Tappan, N.J.: Fleming H. Revell, 1978. (A helpful book on how to deal with sexual dreams, fantasies, and other concerns within the context of Christian faith.)

Wilson, Earl D. *Sexual Sanity: Breaking Free from Uncontrolled Habits.* Downers Grove, Ill.: Inter-Varsity Press, 1984. (A small but excellent book. Wilson is dealing mainly with the issue of the control of sexual obsessions—a welcome emphasis in an anything-goes society. Balanced, well written, and sensitive. His chapter on homosexuality is, I think, particularly well done.)

Brecher, Edward M. *Love, Sex, and Aging: A Consumers Union Report.* Boston: Little, Brown, 1984. (A study of the sexual attitudes and activities of Americans over fifty. Seeks to destroy the stereotype of older people as lonely, unhappy, and sexually inactive. There is no Christian input into this study, but Christians would do well to be apprised of its research.)

Fortune, Marie Marshall. *Sexual Violence: The Unmentionable Sin.* New York: Pilgrim Press, 1983. (A helpful pastoral look at a problem that is more pervasive than most will admit. Fortune contends that "We have not heard about sexual violence in the Church because we have not spoken about it." She suggests ways the minister can show openness to this problem and, as a result, be a genuine agent of help and healing.)

Greer, Germaine. *Sex & Destiny: The Politics of Human Fertility.* New York: Harper & Row, 1984. (Greer is an important feminist writer, and you need to be acquainted with her work. Her first book, *The Female Eunuch*, catapulted her onto the international scene. *Sex and Destiny* is her newest work, and it is a significant effort. The main point of the book is that our attitudes toward sex, reproduction, and children are governed by politics and guided by economics. Her contention is that the West's attempts to force birth control on the Third World is motivated by a desire to maintain political and economic supremacy.)

Keen, Sam. *The Passionate Life: Stages of Loving.* San Francisco: Harper & Row, 1983. (Describes five stages that many go through in the movement to growing maturity: "child," "rebel," "adult," "outlaw," and "mature lover." Although not particularly Christian in its orientation, it nevertheless is a helpful study.)

Ladas, Alice Kahn, Beverly Whipple, and John D. Perry. *The G Spot: And Other Recent Discoveries About Human Sexuality.* New York: Holt, Rinehart and Winston, 1982. (There have been a whole host of studies in human sexuality; this one is mentioned because it is the most recent. In the 1940s we had Kinsey's *Sexual Behavior in the Human Male*; in the 1950s it was his *Sexual Behavior in the Human Female*; in the 1960s we saw Masters and Johnson's *Human Sexual Response*; and in the 1970s *The Hite Report*. This book adds to the tradition. It tells of new research into what is called the Grafenberg spot, a small area within the anterior vaginal wall of women. Proper stimulation of the area seems to bring forth a vaginal orgasm physiologically and psychologically distinct from an ordinary orgasm. This research corresponds to what many women have felt—namely, two different kinds of orgasms.)

Mace, David R. *The Christian Response to the Sexual Revolution*. Nashville: Abingdon Press, 1970. (More than just a reaction, this little book seeks to set Christian sexual ethics within the context of the major cultural shifts in this century. Mace examines the Old Testament world and the early church to separate fact from myth regarding a Christian approach to sex. He shows how some basic misconceptions about sex have, over the centuries, become accepted Christian teaching. In the back is a helpful annotated bibliography of forty books on the subject. You should also be aware that Dr. Mace has written over twenty volumes on the general subjects of sex, marriage, and family. Examples are *Getting Ready for Marriage, Sexual Difficulties in Marriage,* and *Love and Anger in Marriage.*)

Russell, Diana E. H. *Rape in Marriage*. New York: Macmillan, 1982. (An important study on an important subject. The ignorance of this subject is so widespread that as recently as 1979 a California state senator could ask, "But if you can't rape your wife, who can you rape?" If Christians are ever going to lead the way in calling for the full humanity of women, these are the kinds of issues they must deal with.)

Sarrel, Lorna J., and Philip M. Sarrel. *Sexual Turning Points: The Seven Stages of Adult Sexuality*. New York: Macmillan, 1984. (Studying these "seven stages of adult sexuality," the authors are reporting rather than making value judgments, so be prepared for numerous non-Christian concepts. The stages are sexual unfolding, making [or breaking] commitments, marriage, pregnancy, parenting, divorce and remarriage, midlife and beyond.)

Scanzoni, Letha. *Sexuality*. Philadelphia: Westminster Press, 1984. (A small but helpful book on encouraging Christian women to affirm their sexuality.)

HOMOSEXUALITY

Atkinson, David. *Homosexuals in the Christian Fellowship*. Grand Rapids, Mich.: Eerdmans, 1979. (This book provides a good summary of the three main positions on homosexuality and then sets forth a biblical perspective rooted in the Christian doctrine of creation.)

Davidson, Alex. *The Returns of Love*. Downers Grove, Ill.: Inter-Varsity Press, 1970. (This book is composed of a series of letters from the author—who is writing under a pseudonym—to a friend. The author is a deeply committed Christian who is struggling with the deep-seated and all but overwhelming nature of his homosexual desires. He views homosexual *activity* as a transgression of God's law and seeks to be free. Throughout we are allowed to enter the anguish, the loneliness, and the rejection that the homosexual experiences even from the Church.)

Field, David. *The Homosexual Way—A Christian Option?* Downers Grove, Ill.: Inter-Varsity Press, 1979. (This is a brief, 50–page booklet, but it packs a good deal of helpful material into that short space.)

Karlen, Arno. *Sexuality and Homosexuality*. New York: W. W. Norton, 1971. (This book is perhaps a bit dated now, but it is a massive sociological study of homosexuality. In a sense, it seeks to determine whether there is a major sexual revolution afoot in our culture or whether we are seeing instead an important revolution in the scientific study of sex. Arno comes to the latter conclusion and therefore seeks to show that the homosexuality of the past is not significantly different from what we are seeing today.)

Lovelace, Richard F. *Homosexuality and the Church*. Old Tappan, N.J.: Fleming H. Revell, 1978. (A well-argued and helpful book on the homosexual question. Lovelace concludes that the Bible does not support homosexual practice and that practicing homosexuals should not receive ordination. The book is both firm and compassionate.)

McNeill, John J. *The Church and the Homosexual*. Kansas City: Sheed Andrews and McMeel, 1976. (This book is dealing with the homosexual question particularly as it pertains to the Roman Catholic church. It works with the biblical material and church tradition and finally arrives at a position of homosexual acceptance.)

Payne, Leanne. *The Healing of the Homosexual*. Westchester: Crossway Books, 1984. (This slender book—46 pages—is helpful mainly because it expresses great hope for the changing of a homosexual orientation. The "healing of the memories" is utilized throughout as a way by which healing prayer can set people free.)

Scanzoni, Letha, and Virginia Ramey Mollenkott. *Is the Homosexual My Neighbor?: Another Christian View.* San Francisco: Harper & Row, 1978. (The conclusion of this book is that the Bible opposes homosexual lust but not homosexual love that is covenantal. It is a book that will disturb many, but their argument must not be thrown away quickly, for they do take the Bible seriously. Everyone should concur in their concern for a more compassionate and informed stance on the part of the Church toward homosexuals.)

Scroggs, Robin. *The New Testament and Homosexuality.* Philadelphia: Fortress Press, 1983. (In this book Dr. Scroggs seeks to understand the New Testament teaching on homosexuality in light of the Greco-Roman culture, e.g., what cultural issues Paul was dealing with when he wrote his epistles. Scroggs's conclusions may well surprise you. It is a scholarly and readable book.)

Williams, Don. *The Bond That Breaks: Will Homosexuality Split the Church?* Los Angeles: BIM, 1978. (The background that gave rise to this book was the "Task Force Report on Homosexuality" of the United Presbyterian Church, of which Dr. Williams was a member. He takes exception to the majority opinion of the task force, and this book is an attempt to set forth a more conservative view.)

Woods, Richard. *Another Kind of Love.* Chicago: Thomas More Press, 1977. (An attempt by a Catholic writer to forge a homosexual spirituality. The author unapologetically believes that homosexuality is an acceptable life-style for a Christian and seeks to deal with the many practical and pastoral problems such a commitment brings. Least satisfying are his attempts to deal with the biblical data on homosexuality. More helpful is his chapter on "Gay Spirituality," though many [including myself] find the two terms tough to reconcile.)

DIVORCE AND REMARRIAGE

Kysar, Myrna, and Robert Kysar. *The Asundered: Biblical Teachings on Divorce and Remarriage.* Atlanta, Ga.: John Knox Press, 1978. (A very thoughtful book on the Bible's teaching on divorce and remarriage. Covers all relevant biblical data, concentrating particularly on Moses, Jesus, and Paul. It concludes with a chapter that seeks to apply biblical insight to the practical issues faced in local congregations.)

Laney, J. Carl. *The Divorce Myth*. Minneapolis: Bethany House, 1981. (This book takes a firm position against divorce and remarriage. Of special interest is Dr. Laney's interpretation of the "exception clause" in Matthew so as to maintain a consistent "no-divorce" position. This book also contains a bibliography of similar-minded works.)

Mackin, Theodore. *Divorce and Remarriage: Marriage in the Catholic Church*. New York: Paulist Press, 1984. (This is a really substantial history of the divorce/remarriage question in the Roman Catholic church. It begins with the Jewish background through the biblical witness and proceeds right on up to the present time. It considers many major Catholic figures and events on the subject and even has a section on the Protestant Reformers.)

Olsen, V. Norskov. *The New Testament Logia on Divorce*. Tubingen: J. C. B. Mohr, 1971. (An interesting study of the Protestant Reformers' interpretation of the New Testament passages on divorce. Going to primary sources, Olsen surveys such figures as Erasmus, Luther, Zwingli, Calvin, Tyndale, Milton, and others.)

THE SINGLE LIFE

Collins, Gary, ed. *It's O.K. to Be Single*. Waco, Tex.: Word Publishing, 1976. (A helpful collection of essays from the Continental Congress on the Family. Because the relationship of the Church to single people is one of the genuinely crucial issues today, any resource that can be helpful is welcome.)

Goergen, Donald. *The Sexual Celibate*. New York: Seabury Press, 1974. (A really good book that takes head-on the sexuality of celibates in the monastic tradition. The author has a sophisticated grasp of both theology and modern psychology and takes a frank look at such seldom-discussed topics as friendship and intimacy, sexual fantasies and masturbation, homosexuality, etc. Very helpful for monastics and those interested in the monastic tradition.)

Huddleston, Mary Anne, ed. *Celibate Loving: Encounter in Three Dimensions.*. New York: Paulist Press, 1984. (This anthology is a witness to celibacy, especially for those in the Catholic church who are interested in a vow of celibacy. It considers the psychological, spiritual, and social dimensions, with such contributors as John Davanaugh and Henri Nouwen.)

Nouwen, Henri J. M. *Clowning in Rome: Reflections on Solitude, Celibacy, Prayer, and Contemplation.* Garden City, N.Y.: Image Books, 1979. (This valuable book has a helpful chapter entitled "Celibacy and the Holy.")

Swindoll, Luci. *Wide My World, Narrow My Bed.* Portland, Oreg.: Multnomah Press, 1982. (This book is an enjoyable tribute to the single life as a good and fulfilling choice.)

MARRIAGE

Achtemeier, Elizabeth. *The Committed Marriage.* Philadelphia: Westminster Press, 1976. (The best single book for those who are prepared to enter into the vow of fidelity as I have sought to describe it. The author sees Christian marriage as a form of discipleship and deals effectively with fidelity, divorce, the role of women, and much more. Must reading.)

Arnold, Heini. *In the Image of God: Marriage and Chastity in Christian Life.* Rifton, N.Y.: Plough Publishing House, 1977. (A series of talks given by one of the leaders [recently deceased] of the Bruderhof Community. The talks were given as a preparation for several weddings that were to occur in their fellowship. While not particularly profound, the comments are nevertheless a strong indictment of society's obsession with sex and a call to a more sane and balanced perspective.)

Bird, Joseph W., and Louis F. Bird. *The Freedom of Sexual Love.* Garden City, N.Y.: Doubleday, 1967. (A book written to help Catholics develop a healthy Christian concept of sexuality in marriage. Its scope, therefore, is limited, but within that context it is helpful. As expected, it takes a traditional Catholic view on birth control.)

Dennehy, Raymond. *Christian Married Love.* San Francisco: Ignatius Press, 1981. (A series of five contributions—from Malcolm Muggeridge to Louis Bouyer—on Christian married love. Three of the essays deal directly with *Humanae Vitae.* Though in one sense this is a specifically Catholic issue, Protestants really do need to think through Muggeridge's contention that the rejection of *Humanae Vitae* will "lead inevitably, as night follows day, to abortion and then to euthanasia" [p. 27].)

Howell, John C. *Equality and Submission in Marriage.* Nashville: Broadman Press, 1979. (One of the most helpful things about this little book is the thoughtful discussion of the relevant Scripture passages. Also helpful is the careful footnoting, which can lead the serious student to many good sources. Though coming to a clear position on the authority/submission issue, Dr. Howell encourages each couple to work through a marriage style that is suitable for each partner and that honors Christ.)

LaHaye, Tim, and Beverly LaHaye. *The Act of Marriage: The Beauty of Sexual Love.* Grand Rapids, Mich.: Zondervan, 1976. (Very simplistic and sometimes erroneous, this is nevertheless a book you should be aware of because of its considerable popularity.)

McGinnis, Alan Loy. *The Romance Factor.* New York: Harper & Row, 1982. (A vigorous testimony to the tremendous potential of monogamous romance and marriage. Well written and thoughtful, it continues the tradition of the author's earlier, well-received book, *The Friendship Factor.*)

Penner, Clifford, and Joyce Penner. *The Gift of Sex: A Christian Guide to Sexual Fulfillment.* Waco, Tex.: Word, 1981. (One of the very best books on human sexuality from an unapologetic Christian perspective. Although it contains good sections on the spiritual and emotional aspects of sexuality, its largest contribution is in its excellent discussion of the physical dimension. It is genuinely gratifying to find a book that avoids the silliness of many sex manuals and instead provides mature and frank guidance. Must reading.)

Petersen, J. Allan. *The Myth of the Greener Grass.* Wheaton, Ill.: Tyndale House, 1983. (A thoughtful and readable book that faces head-on the matter of infidelity in marriage. As well as destroying the many myths about sexual infidelity, it contains a helpful chapter on how to "Affair-Proof Your Marriage." Recommended reading.)

Shedd, Charlie, and Martha Shedd. *Celebration in the Bedroom.* Waco, Tex.: Word, 1979. (Shedd is another writer you need to know. He began in 1965 with *Letters to Karen*, letters he had written to his daughter on how to keep love in marriage. *Letters to Phillip* was an attempt to do the same thing for his son. *Promises to Peter* was his counsel on child rearing. In *The Stork Is Dead* he forced Christians to think seriously about such matters as birth control and masturbation. He has really been a pioneer in the Christian world in the areas of sex, marriage, and family. *Celebration in the Bedroom* is, of course, an effort to help us affirm our sexuality in a Christian context. Don't let his breezy style fool you—behind it all is careful thinking.)

Swindoll, Charles R. *Strike the Original Match.* Portland, Oreg.: Multnomah Press, 1980. (A helpful book on building a stronger marriage. Swindoll brings a pastoral heart to his writing, and we can be grateful for his wide acceptance and influence. Swindoll has also written three little booklets related to sex: *Sensuality, Singleness,* and *Divorce.*)

Trobisch, Walter. *I Married You.* New York: Harper & Row, 1971. (Helpful counsel on marriage, couched in the context of a weekend teaching session.)

Wheat, Ed, and Gaye Wheat. *Intended for Pleasure.* Rev. ed. Old Tappan, N.J.: Fleming H. Revell, 1981. (An easy-to-read reference book on sex in marriage presented within the framework of biblical teaching. It covers a variety of topics, such as premature ejaculation, frigidity, impotence, sexual intimacy, sex during pregnancy, etc.)

Part III
Power

Chapter 10   Destructive Power

Nothing can destroy like power that is divorced from the kingdom of God.

READINGS

AN ESCALATION OF POWER

The powerful always find it harder and harder to put up with resistance to their power; they become more and more capable of crushing all resistance, and so become more and more powerful. . . . This is true not only of individuals and commercial firms, but also of humanity as a whole, which has for several centuries been committed because of its technological progress to an escalation of power, spiralling inexorably upward. Will the whole adventure end in catastrophe? This is what a growing number of thinkers are asking.

—Paul Tournier

THE POWERS ARE INCARNATED

For the powers are *incarnated* in very concrete forms, and their power is expressed in institutions or organizations. We cannot think of the battle as only a spiritual one. The *exousia* of the state is incarnated in a government, in the police force, the army. . . . The spiritual warfare we are summoned to is concerned with human realities—with injustice, oppression, authoritarianism, the domination of the state by money, the exaltation of sex or science, etc.

—Jacques Ellul

THE DISCERNMENT OF SPIRITS

When Paul lists (1 Corinthians 12:8–10) the various gifts of the Spirit which are bestowed upon the church, he names among them the "discernment of spirits." In the church the distinction becomes clear between movings of spirits which are of and unto God and those which are of and unto the evil one. This involves especially the discerning of the Powers which hold the hearts and actions of men under their sway in specific times and places.

—Hendrik Berkhof

THE TECHNICO-SCIENTIFIC COMMANDMENT

From science, technology was born, and its present vogue likewise has its source in the myth of power. Combined in it are the power of knowledge and the power of money. Technology, the fruit of knowledge, procures economic power. This gives it its primacy in the modern world. "The only categorical imperative which is still effective and universally obeyed," writes René Gillouin, "is the technico-scientific commandment: Thou shalt invent, thou shalt apply, thou shalt above all things create power, without concerning thyself in the least with the use which will be made of it. . . . As if power were the supreme value."

—Paul Tournier

THE CONQUEST OF THE PRINCIPALITIES

The conquest of the principalities by Jesus Christ has, indeed, wrought a fundamental change in the state of the world. . . . It is not by accident that the spirit of evil is growing more frenzied, for Jesus has broken its power, and this realization inspires panic.

—Heinrich Schlier

DAILY SCRIPTURE READINGS

Sunday: Christ the Creator of the Powers / Colossians 1:15–20
Monday: The Powers Limited in Knowledge / 1 Corinthians 2:6–8
Tuesday: The Elemental Spirits / Colossians 2:20–23
Wednesday: The Prince of the Power of the Air / Ephesians 2:1–2
Thursday: Christ Disarmed the Powers / Colossians 2:8–15
Friday: Christ Exalted Above the Powers / Ephesians 1:19–23
Saturday: Our Warfare Against the Powers / Ephesians 6:12–18

STUDY QUESTIONS

1. In your own words, how would you describe the power that destroys?

2. What was the sin of Simon Magnus? In what ways do you see it evidenced today?

3. Why is there seemingly always such a close connection between pride and destructive power?

4. If Christ created the powers, how can they be in revolt? Did the fall affect them, or was there a fall of the powers prior to the human fall?

5. What do you think about the notion that the principalities and powers can impact not just individuals but institutions and whole structures of society? Can you think of

any biblical examples in which institutions are viewed in this light?

6. The Church has been given the responsibility of discerning the powers. Are there ways to encourage this ministry in your church?

7. What do you think of the idea of technology as a power?

8. What modern-day powers would you list?

9. The Bible tells us that Christ disarmed the powers and triumphed over them. In what ways have you seen this to be true in your own experience? Are there ways in which it is yet to be accomplished?

10. Do you think the weapons of Ephesians 6 are strong, or weak, when it comes to dealing with the "real" world of totalitarianism and oppression?

CREATIVE SERENDIPITIES

SERENDIPITY #1

"If with Christ you died to the elemental spirits of the universe, why do you live as if you still belonged to the world? Why do you submit to regulations, 'Do not handle, Do not taste, Do not touch'?" (Col. 2:20–21).

To the Christians in Galatia, Paul counseled; "For freedom Christ has set us free; stand fast therefore, and do not submit again to a yoke of slavery" (Gal. 5:1). Discuss together ways in which the Church, in its concern for moral purity, has stifled the gospel liberty we have in Christ. Why is legalism such a problem in the Church? Is there a good side to legalism?

Now, discuss ways in which both gospel liberty and moral purity can be maintained. Are there dangers in the proposals you are developing? The spiritual life involves risks, but if we understand the risks we are better equipped to deal with them.

If you are in a group be especially sensitive to the feelings of each member. Some may have chosen legalism because it is "safe." They need our love and support to know that God has not given us "the spirit of fear, but of power, and of love, and of a sound mind" (2 Tim. 1:7, KJV). Others may have reveled in the liberty they have in the gospel and turned it into "an opportunity for the flesh" (Gal. 5:13). If repentance and confession comes, we receive it reverently, compassionately. Close the session with prayer.

SERENDIPITY #2

"Put on the whole armor of God, that you may be able to stand againsts the wiles of the devil" (Eph. 6:11).

The apostle Paul described our spiritual arsenal within the context of the first-century Roman army. Your task is to do the same thing using the context of the twentieth-century business world. Think through the actual list Paul gives—truth, righteousness, peace, faith, salvation, the Spirit (the Word of God), and prayer. But remember that Paul was not trying to be exhaustive in his list, so consider any specifics you might add in the fight of faith today.

After you have finished, gather together in prayer for the arming of one another for your fight of faith.

Chapter 11 Creative Power

Under the redeeming love of Christ, power becomes creative and life-giving.

READINGS

JESUS AND POWER

Thinking thus about the way Jesus acted, it comes to me that the key to the problem of violence is to be found in that of power: that benign violence is that which is put at the service of others, protecting the weak, healing the sick, liberating the exploited, fighting the injustice of the powerful; and that improper violence is violence on one's own behalf, aimed at securing power for oneself, violence which is inspired by the fascination of power.

—Paul Tournier

PRAYER AS A WORK OF POWER

The call to prayer is not an invitation to retreat to a familiar piety, but a challenge to make a radical move toward prayer as "the only necessary thing" (Luke 10:42). In prayer about the nuclear crisis, we discover a dimension of prayer not seen before, a dimension that becomes visible precisely in the confrontation with the power and principalities.

—Henri J. M. Nouwen

DISCIPLINE

The spirit assents when Jesus bids us love our enemies, but flesh and blood are too strong and prevent our carrying it out. Therefore we have to practise strictest daily discipline; only so can the flesh learn the painful lesson that it has no rights of its own. Regular daily prayer is a great help here, and so is daily meditation on the Word of God and every kind of bodily discipline and asceticism.

—Dietrich Bonhoeffer

A POWER TO DEFEAT POWER

There is a power . . . of which Jesus approves; that is the power he promises to give his disciples. Jesus gives his followers a spiritual power to overcome evil, to resist temptation, to serve him—a power to defeat power. There is no personal merit to be gained from it. It comes from God and can be removed by God.

—Cheryl Forbes

SPEAKING TRUTH TO POWER

And so when I came before him [Oliver Cromwell] I was moved to say, "Peace be on this house"; and I bid him keep in the fear of God that he might receive wisdom, that by it he might be ordered, that with it he might order all things under his hand to God's glory. And I spake much to him of Truth. . . . And many more words I had with him. . . . And as I was turning he catched me by the hand and said these words with tears in his eyes, "Come again to my house; for if thou and I were but an hour in a day together we should be nearer one to the other."

—George Fox

DAILY SCRIPTURE READINGS

Sunday: Moses Empowered for Service / Exodus 3:11–14

Monday:	Power to Bring Unity / Acts 15:1–29
Tuesday:	The Character of Creative Power / Matthew 5:1–12
Wednesday:	The Mark of Love / 1 John 4:7–14
Thursday:	Freedom as a Mark of Power / Galatians 5:1–15
Friday:	The Mark of Humility / Matthew 23:8–12
Saturday:	The Power to be Faithful / Hebrews 11:35–38

STUDY QUESTIONS

1. Do you think it is possible for a person to exercise a ministry of creative power outside a spiritual life?

2. Moses had to go into the desert before he could learn about God's power. Do we need to experience our own "deserts" before we can really know God's power?

3. What do you think of Jeremiah's ministry? Would you like to have been in his shoes? Is there anything today that compares to Israel's belief in the invincibility of Zion?

4. Consider the cross of Christ as the apex of the power that creates. It did not look like power when Jesus was dying, yet God made it the greatest of power. Are there things today that do not look like power and yet can be seen with the eye of faith to be true power?

5. What are the marks of power mentioned in the book? Are there other characteristics of true power that you would have added?

6. Could we do without any of these marks of power and still have true spiritual power?

7. I suggest that self-control embraces both self-esteem and self-denial. Do you agree or disagree? Can you have genuine self-esteem without self-denial?

8. How have you seen power used in the home in a life-

giving way? Have you seen times when power has been used destructively?

9. What are things you can do to enhance communication in your marriage?

10. What can you do to nurture the right use of spiritual power in your church? Are there ways to minimize the use of destructive power?

CREATIVE SERENDIPITIES

SERENDIPITY #1

"This I command you, to love one another" (John 15:17).

The issue of power touches us at the point of our relationships, so in this serendipity we want to experience the power of Christ in the healing and strengthening of relationships. Begin by reading John 15:12–17. Jesus said these words when he was in the upper room with the disciples. Have a period of silence following the reading to allow the words of Scripture to dwell richly in your hearts.

Now, in your imagination have your friends and acquaintances pass by you. Begin with those in your home, then your neighbors, those in your church, and finally those at your place of employment. As each one passes by, inwardly breathe a prayer of thanksgiving for him or her. Do not feel rushed: you may want to take fifteen or twenty minutes to complete this little task. The idea is to relish and enjoy the many wonderful relationships God has brought into your life.

Next, ask the Lord to show you two or three in that vast group whom you could love more. Do not try to think of people you hate, because it could well be that you do not "hate" any of them. But I am sure there are some that you could love a little more.

Once you have singled out the two or three you would like to love more, think of them one at a time and bless them in the name of the Lord. Do not try to have more love for them—that would be self-defeating—just bless them. Ask God to give them a good day. Perhaps you might pray that they will meet someone today who is a special encouragement to them, or that they will begin reading an enjoyable and uplifting book. The idea is to seek their good in prayer. In your imagination shake their hand or wish them a good day. Have the leader close the meeting with prayer for the healing of all broken relationships.

SERENDIPITY #2

For freedom Christ has set us free" (Gal. 5:1).

God intends that power be used for the good of others. In this experience we want to celebrate the use of power to release people to enjoy God and to love him forever. Begin by reading John 11:17–44, the story of the raising of Lazarus from the dead. Try to enter into the feelings of Martha as she talked with Jesus. Then center your attention on Jesus' words to Martha, "I am the resurrection and the life; he who believes in me, though he die, yet shall he live, and whoever lives and believes in me shall never die" (John 11:25–26). Allow the reality of these words to enter your heart and set you free.

Next, turn your attention to the resurrection of Lazarus. Try to see and hear the event. Enter the excitement of the moment when Lazarus came out of the tomb with the gravecloths wound around his arms and legs. Perhaps you will want to turn to Jesus and worship him and thank him for this display of kingdom power.

Now, center on Jesus' words to the crowd, "Unbind him, and let him go" (John 11:44). In a mighty act of power, Jesus brought Lazarus back from the dead, but the people were also given a work to do—to release Lazarus from his burial cloths.

We, you see, have a part to play in Christ's ministry of liberation. Ask God to show you people in your world that need release from the "gravecloths." Perhaps they have been touched by God in a significant way, but they still are bound and need your ministry of releasing. See if God doesn't give you a specific act of "unbinding" that you can perform for them in the next few days. Maybe one of your children is frightened by a new situation at school, and by taking him or her out to breakfast to talk about it you could engage in the ministry of releasing. Perhaps a work associate could be freed by a word of encouragement. Maybe your spouse needs your expression of love and concern. These are all acts of power that liberate. Be faithful to any guidance you are given. Close by singing the hymn "O for a Thousand Tongues to Sing."

Chapter 12 The Ministry of Power

We are called to the joyful life of power for the sake of others.

READINGS

POWER IS GIVEN

Power is given: it is an inevitable reality in the world in which we live. Power itself is not evil. The use of certain forms of power or the abuse of power is where several questions arise. Exploitative and manipulative power are forms of power that are incongruent with the Gospel because they are power over others. Nutrient and integrative power are congruent with the Gospel precisely because they are forms of power at the service of others.

—James McNamara

THE POWER THAT LIVES ON

The power that lives on is the real power, the inner power: the power to move mountains, to tame the animals and bring them back, as St. Francis did, to the human family, the power to charm men to holiness not by what is said merely but by the voice that says it, the personality it expresses. You find a hint or likeness of this power in all the really great: in the men of genius, perhaps, in the great lovers of humanity, in those who are filled with the love of a purpose greater than themselves; but you find it in its fullness in the saints, whose power is more than human since it is the life of the Spirit within them.

—Gerald Vann

THE NATURE OF SPIRITUAL POWER

Spiritual power . . . resides entirely within the individual and has nothing to do with the capacity to coerce others. People of great spiritual power may be wealthy and may upon occasion occupy political positions of leadership, but they are as likely to be poor and lacking in political authority. Then, what is the capacity of spiritual power if not the capacity to coerce? It is the capacity to make decisions with maximum awareness. It is consciousness.

—M. Scott Peck

SPIRITUAL POWER GONE BAD

I always remember a worthy pastor, apparently humble and shy, who had brought his sick wife to see me. As I was beginning to question his wife, asking her what the trouble was and how it had begun, the husband interrupted me impatiently: "It's quite simple, doctor. I have the Holy Spirit and my wife has not." . . . I was astonished. It really is terrible for a sick woman to hear her husband pass such a wounding and unjust judgment upon her. I felt as much pity for the husband as for the patient. Poor man! He was certainly sincere. No doubt he had had a genuine experience of the gift of the Holy Spirit; and it had so intoxicated him that, modest though he was by nature, it had given him a sense of superiority and power that had quite blinded him. He had no notion of the harm that he was doing to his wife.

—Paul Tournier

Love is a power that flows into persons and drives them to move toward others. Love enables people to do loving sorts of things and be loving sorts of persons. That love is a power explains why Paul personifies it, talking as if love itself did things. Love believes, he says. And love endures, hopes, and bears all things. What he obviously means is that love is the power which enables people to endure, to believe, and to hope.

—Lewis B. Smedes

DAILY SCRIPTURE READINGS

Sunday: Jesus' Ministry of Power / Matthew 4:23–25

Monday: Jesus' Refusal to Use Power / Matthew 4:1–11

Tuesday: The Promise of Power / Acts 1:8

Wednesday: Not Talk But Power / 1 Corinthians 4:19–20

Thursday: Power Over the Tongue / James 3:6–12

Friday: Power Over the Passions / 1 John 2:15–17

Saturday: Power Over the Mind / Philippians 4:8

STUDY QUESTIONS

1. What strikes you the most about Jesus' ministry of power?

2. I say that spiritual power can function with or without official human authorization. What do you think? Is official authorization a help, or a hindrance, to the ministry of power?

3. How important is "hidden preparation" to the ministry of power? Have you seen people who have tried to exer-

cise spiritual power without hidden preparation? What is the result of their work?

4. In the midst of your busy world, what are some ways you can experience hidden preparation?

5. Why would the ministry of small things be a necessary prerequisite to the work of power? Are "small things" always "big things" in the kingdom of God?

6. Is the ministry of power a "big deal" to you?

7. Is the idea of power's aloneness new to you? Does it resonate with your experience?

8. How important is solitude to "do battle with the Devil"?

9. Do you think God always heals the body if we are truly exercising a ministry of power?

10. Can you think of any specific ways you could exercise the ministry of power with reference to the State?

CREATIVE SERENDIPITIES

SERENDIPITY #1

"Therefore, since we are surrounded by so great a cloud of witnesses . . ." (Heb. 12:1).

Choose two people that you feel displayed spiritual power through their ministry; one from the Bible and one from Church history. For example, you might choose the apostle Paul and John Wesley, or perhaps Esther and Saint Teresa. Begin by discussing the various ways power was exhibited through each one. Note the different issues each faced and how they dealt with them. What similarities do you see between the two? What differences do you find? List the marks of power you discover.

Now try to imagine these men or women in your shoes. If they worked at your job and faced the issues you face, how would they do it? What would they say? How would they respond to difficult situations? What decisions would they make?

You are a unique person, and no one would want you to slavishly imitate someone else, no matter how great, but does watching them walk in your shoes give you any insight into your task? Are there ways you can be a minister of power? Close the session by affirming one another's special giftedness.

SERENDIPITY #2

"And he went about all Galilee, teaching in their synagogues and preaching the gospel of the kingdom and healing every disease and every infirmity among the people" (Matt. 4:23).

Contemplate Jesus' ministry of power. Think about the times he healed the sick and gave sight to the blind. Reflect on how he forgave sins. Remember his tenderness when he dealt with the bruised and broken in spirit. Think about his love and compassion.

Now draw near to him in prayer. Become aware of his love and acceptance. Are there things within you that need his powerful touch? He is willing to come in if you will open the door. In the silence, invite him to touch you at the point of your need. Then give thanks.

Chapter 13 The Vow of Service

The destructive bid for power is answered in the vow of service which in turn forms the foundation upon which true spiritual power can function.

READINGS

THE SERVICE OF ACTIVE HELPFULNESS

The second service that one should perform for another in a Christian community is that of active helpfulness. This means, initially, simple assistance in trifling, external matters.There is a multitude of these things wherever people live together. Nobody is too good for the meanest service. One who worries about the loss of time that such petty, outward acts of helpfulness entail is usually taking the importance of his own career too solemnly.

—Dietrich Bonhoeffer

THE INSTITUTION AS SERVANT

This is my thesis: caring for persons, the more able and the less able serving each other, is the rock upon which a good society is built. Whereas, until recently, caring was largely person-to-person, now most of it is mediated through institutions—often large, complex, powerful, impersonal, not always competent, sometimes corrupt. If a better society is to be built, one that is more just and more loving, one that provides greater creative opportunity for its people, then the most open course is to *raise both the capacity to serve and the very performance as servant* of existing major institutions by new regenerative forces operating within them.

—Robert K. Greenleaf

THERE IS A SPIRIT WHICH I FEEL

There is a spirit which I feel that delights to do no evil, nor to revenge any wrong, but delights to endure all things, in hope to enjoy its own in the end. Its hope is to outlive all wrath and contention, and to weary out all exaltation and cruelty, or whatever is of a nature contrary to itself. It sees to the end of all temptations. As it bears no evil in itself, so it conceives none in thoughts to any other. If it be betrayed, it bears it, for its ground and spring is the mercies and forgiveness of God.

—James Nayler

POWER THROUGH SERVING

Even though the community knows that "all power both in heaven and on earth has been given" (Matt. 28:18) to the risen one as God's "representative," and that all heavenly and earthly "powers" must bow the knee before him (Phil. 2:10–11), it nevertheless participates in such power only *by serving.*

—Martin Hengel

A SERVANT GOD

Our God is a servant God. It is difficult for us to comprehend that we are liberated by someone who became powerless, that we are being strengthened by someone who became weak, that we find new hope in someone who divested himself of all distinctions, and

98

that we find a leader in someone who became a servant.
—Donald P. McNeill, Douglas A. Morrison, Henri J.
M. Nouwen

DAILY SCRIPTURE READINGS

Sunday: The Gentiles Lord It over Them / Matthew 20:25–28
Monday: The Ministry of the Towel / John 13:3–17
Tuesday: The Mind of Christ / Philippians 2:5–8
Wednesday: The Service of Love / 1 Corinthians 13:1–7
Thursday: The Ministry of Small Things / Luke 3:10–14
Friday: Service in the Family / Ephesians 5:21–6:9
Saturday: The Acts of Service / Romans 12:9–21

STUDY QUESTIONS

1. Could you give a one-sentence definition of the vow of service?

2. How is the old monastic vow of obedience related to the vow of service?

3. What does it mean to submit to the ways of God?

4. Should we always submit to spiritual leaders? Do we serve people by submitting to them, or are there times when we serve them by refusing to submit?

5. Out of your experience, what examples can you give of parents who really served their children in a healthy way?

6. Do you think honorific titles—Doctor, Reverend, Professor—are consistent with Jesus' emphasis upon servanthood?

7. Is there anyone in your experience that you could specif-

ically name as an "articulator of inner events"? How did he or she come to have that capacity?

8. What particular problems have you encountered in your vocation when you have sought to be a servant?

9. Are there positions in the business world that are not appropriate for the servant leadership model?

10. How could a new Christian movement that incorporates the vows of simplicity, fidelity, and service begin in our day?

CREATIVE SERENDIPITIES

SERENDIPITY #1

If I then, your Lord and Teacher, have washed your feet, you also ought to wash one another's feet. For I have given you an example, that you also should do as I have done to you" (John 13:14–15).

In the first century, footwashing was a way of serving people by meeting a genuine need. People had cracked and dirty feet. It was also an act of genuine humility, for this was a job reserved for the lower end of the pecking order. Keeping these things in mind, we want in this session to discover ways to "wash one another's feet."

Give every person a three-by-five card. Then divide into groups of two and have people visit with each other with an eye to discovering some specific act of service that would help to meet a genuine need. After a time of visiting, every person should go off alone. Write down the name of the person you have visited with and the specific task you feel would be a genuine act of service to that person. It could be something as simple as baking cookies or mowing the lawn. After this is done, the group leader collects all the cards, mixes them, and then allows people to pick out cards randomly. Over the next week or two prayerfully consider the possibility of actually doing the task noted for the person named on the card. We do not want this to be artificial, so if the suggestion does not feel appropriate to you, drop it. But even if the specific suggestion is not followed, the exercise will help to sensitize group members to ways of living in service toward each other.

SERENDIPITY #2

"Love one another with brotherly affection; outdo one another in showing honor" (Romans 12:10).

In this experience we want to explore how your church can become even more of a servant institution than it is now. Begin by listing on a blackboard or a large sheet of paper every way you feel your church now functions as a servant institution. How does it serve its members? How does it serve the community? How does it serve the outcasts of society? How does it serve the world? List only those things that your church is now doing, not the things you wish it were doing. Every fellowship of Christians, no matter how imperfect, is engaged in many acts of service, and we often overlook these sacrificial efforts. When you have finished, look over this list and thank God for the many good things that are being done in the name of Christ.

Now draw up another list of the areas in which you feel genuine servanthood is hindered in your church. This is not a gripe session; strictly forbid public criticism of the pastors or other designated leaders in the church. Focus on structural or procedural patterns rather than on individuals. For example, you may feel that the "family emphasis" of your church makes it difficult to effectively serve the single adult. Or you may feel that a new "wineskin" is needed to respond to the needs of the handicapped. You will think of many more ideas.

Now, look over your list. Some of the ideas, though

valid and good, are beyond the resources of your church and cannot be realistically undertaken. Others, for one reason or another, may not fit into the mission and purpose of your particular church. But hopefully there are several ideas that are attainable and should be implemented. Decide on what resources are needed to accomplish these things, and assign individual responsibilities for getting the job done before you end the meeting. Remember, one simple act of service rendered is better than ten wonderful ideas that are merely discussed. Close with a prayer of commission for all who have been given specific tasks to accomplish.

BOOKS ON POWER

The books in this section have been organized into the following categories:

The Modern Search for Power

Biblical and Theological Studies

The Principalities and Powers Today

Power and the Business World

Power and Compassion

THE MODERN SEARCH FOR POWER

Aronson, Steven M. L. *Hype.* New York: William Morrow, 1983. (Shows how modern American superstars manipulate their image in order to exercise power.)

Campolo, Anthony, Jr. *The Power Delusion.* Wheaton, Ill.: Victor Books, 1983. (A simple yet helpful study of power and what a Christian world view has to say about it.)

Forbes, Cheryl. *The Religion of Power.* Grand Rapids, Mich.: Zondervan, 1983. (Attempts to critique the negative influence of power, particularly upon Christians.)

Janeway, Elizabeth. *Powers of the Weak.* New York: Knopf, 1980. (Written by a leader in the women's movement, this book seeks to re-examine the nature and uses of power not in terms of the strong but in terms of the powerless, especially women. Of particular interest is her section on "impractical politics.")

Kissinger, Henry. *Years of Upheaval.* Boston: Little, Brown, 1982. (Kissinger provides us with an intriguing study of power in this book. He himself is well acquainted with the inner workings of power, and the Nixon years provide a rare look at power in all its ruthlessness. Whatever your political outlook, you will find Kissinger an astute observer of the function of power in the political arena.)

Korda, Michael. *Power! How to Get It, How to Use It.* New York: Balantine Books, 1975. (In this book Korda simply brings into the open the power games of modern society—games that all of us play and most of us try to hide, even from ourselves. Though in other cultures the symbols of power are very obvious—crowns and scepters in tribal cultures, bars and stars in the army, for example—modern technological America's power symbols are more hidden and subtle. Korda exposes them all—from corner offices to Gucci shoes. This is no book to scorn; it is filled with significant perceptions about contemporary culture. Obviously, the servant way of Christ is opposed to the world's games of power, so the insights of this book provide real help in knowing where to say no to a world obsessed with power.)

―――. *Success!* New York: Random House, 1977. (A thoroughgoing Machiavellian approach to power in the business world. It frankly and unapologetically embraces greed, ambition, and manipulation as success techniques. You may also want to be aware of how much the Church has bought into the same mentality.)

Nietzsche, Friedrich. *The Will to Power: An Attempted Transvaluation of All Values.* Edited by Oscar Levy. Vol. II, books II and IV. Trans. by Anthony M. Ludovici. New York: Russell & Russell, 1964. (Discussions of the power issue certainly did not begin with Nietzsche, but his writings were something of a watershed on the issue. His works are bold and brazen even for our day—think of the stir he must have caused in the nineteenth century. In *The Will to Power* Nietzsche argues that everything—science, nature, individuals, everything—is motivated and controlled by "the will to power.")

Peck, M. Scott. *People of the Lie: The Hope for Healing Human Evil.* New York: Simon & Schuster, 1983. (A study of the power and the self-deceptive nature of evil and how people can be set free from it.)

——. *The Road Less Traveled.* New York: Simon & Schuster, 1978. (This is Peck's first book, and it has an especially good chapter on the nature of power.)

Ringer, Robert J. *Looking Out for Number One.* Los Angeles: Los Angeles Book Corp.; dist. by Funk & Wagnalls, New York, 1977. (A very humorous book on egocentricity.)

——. *Winning Through Intimidation.* Los Angeles: Los Angeles Book Co., 1973. (A thoroughly pagan and terribly honest look at how to make it big in modern society.)

Snow, C. P. *Corridors of Power.* New York: Scribner's, 1964. (This is a novel about "high" political power. The setting is the British Parliament in the mid-1950s, but that is not the significant thing—it could just as well have been set in first-century Rome or seventeenth-century France. The point is that this novel helps us struggle with the complexities and ambiguities of power in the context of real-life situations.)

Trahey, Jane. *On Women & Power: Who's Got It? How to Get It?* New York: Rawson Associates, 1977. (Coming out of the feminist movement, this book seeks to help women learn how to get and keep what men have had all along—power. This book makes no pretense at being Christian; it is a tough, uncompromising apologetic for "the ultimate power trip!")

BIBLICAL AND THEOLOGICAL STUDIES

Berkhof, Hendrick. *Christ and the Powers.* Trans. by John H. Yoder. Scottdale, Penn.: Herald Press, 1962. (A brief study, but it contains more information than most books four times its size. The finest single study I know of on Paul's teaching on the "powers" [*exousia*]. Essential reading.)

Burkholder, John Richard, and Calvin Redekop, eds. *Kingdom Cross and Community.* Scottdale, Penn.: Herald Press, 1976. (A series of Mennonite essays in honor of Guy F. Hershberger. Contains several good essays on the power question from an Anabaptist tradition, such as "Institutions, Power, and the Gospel" and "The State and the Free Church.")

Caird, G. B. *Principalities and Powers: A Study in Pauline Theology.* Oxford: Clarendon Press, 1956. (A small but perceptive book that was first given as a series of lectures at Queens University in Ontario, Canada. The author seeks to understand

Paul's theology of spiritual powers and the cultural context out of which these convictions developed.)

Carr, Wesley. *Angels and Principalities.* Cambridge: Cambridge University Press, 1981. (Originally a doctoral dissertation, this is a technical study of the Pauline phrase "the angels and the principalities." It covers the background to Paul's thought, the specific texts themselves, and the view of some of the early church fathers.)

Cullmann, Oscar. *The State in the New Testament.* New York: Scribner's, 1956. (Works on the social dimension of power, i.e., government. Studies the relationship between Jesus and the Zealot movement and Jesus and the Roman state. It also looks at the relationship between Paul and the state and the attitude of the Book of Revelation toward the state. It contains a helpful concluding study of the "powers" [*exousia*] in Romans 13:1.)

Hengel, Martin. *Christ and Power.* Philadelphia: Fortress Press, 1977. (A good survey of the power issue from antiquity to the Protestant Reformation. The chapter on Jesus and the powers of his time is especially good. Of particular interest is his contention that Luther saw the power issue for Christians in terms of service.)

Macgregor, G. H. C. "Principalities and Powers: The Cosmic Background of Paul's Thought." *New Testament Studies* (September 1954), pp. 15–28. (A scholarly and helpful exegesis of Paul's use of "principalities and powers.")

Nee, Watchman. *Spiritual Authority.* New York: Christian Fellowship Publishers, 1972. (A study of authority and submission throughout the Bible.)

Schlier, Heinrich. *Principalities and Powers in the New Testament.* Silver Spring, Md.: Herder & Herder, 1961. (A very helpful little book in giving Christians an overall understanding of the New Testament perspective on spiritual powers. I was especially glad for the inclusion of Chapter 2, "Jesus Christ and the Principalities," since the Gospels are often ignored in studies of the principalities and powers.)

Stringfellow, William. *The Politics of Spirituality.* Philadelphia: Westminister Press, 1984. (Stringfellow has never been one to mince words, and this book is true to that reputation. He places spirituality right in the middle of the social arena and shows how God stands in judgment of all human activity.)

Wink, Walter. *Naming the Powers.* Philadelphia: Fortress Press, 1984.

(This book is the first in a three-volume series dealing with the powers in the New Testament. The research is substantial, and the insights are powerful. The best work so far on a long neglected topic. You may find it a bit ponderous at times, but the treasures you will discover are well worth the effort to dig them out.)

Yates, Roy. "The Powers of Evil in the New Testament." *The Evangelical Quarterly*, vol. 52, no. 2 (April/June 1980), pp. 97–111. (This is a scholarly essay on the various terms used in the New Testament to deal with the reality of evil—i.e., principalities, authorities, powers, dominions, thrones, etc. You do not need to know Greek to gain helpful insights from this essay.)

Yoder, John Howard. *The Politics of Jesus*. Grand Rapids, Mich.: Eerdmans, 1972. (This landmark book is helpful in many ways, but three chapters in particular discuss the issue of power: "Christ and Power," "Revolutionary Subordination," and "Let Every Soul Be Subject: Romans 13 and the Authority of the State.")

THE PRINCIPALITIES AND POWERS TODAY

Barth, Karl. *The Christian Life*. Trans. by Geoffrey W. Bromiley. Grand Rapids, Mich.: Eerdmans, 1981. (This is material taken from Barth's *Dogmatics*—a fragment of volume 4, chapter 4. It contains a section entitled "The Lordless Powers," which is very good. In that section he gives considerable attention to mammon as a power.)

Broad, William and Nicholas Wade. *Betrayers of the Truth: Fraud and Deceit in the Halls of Science.*. New York: Simon & Schuster, 1982. (This book demonstrates that scientists are not immune to the temptations of fraud and corruption. The book opens a window for us into the halls of scientific research, where we see the power struggles of ordinary human beings.)

Conway, J. S. *The Nazi Persecution of the Churches 1933–45*. New York: Basic Books, 1968. (This book is of far more than historical interest. It is a study of the state as a demonic power and the Church's inability to discern the true situation.)

Eller, Vernard. *War and Peace from Genesis to Revelation*. Rev. ed. Scottdale, Penn.: Herald Press, 1981. (A readable book on how Christians are to contend with militarism.)

Ellul, Jacques. *The Technological Society*. New York: Knopf, 1970. (A very careful analysis of the domination of "technique" in the modern world by the famous French Christian and sociologist who gave us books like *The Political Illusion*. *The Technological Society* helps to place technology within the context of the larger question of purpose and values.)

———. *Violence: Reflections from a Christian Perspective*. New York: Seabury Press, 1969. (A serious critique of the normal options of pacifism, just war, and a theology of revolution. He then points to a new way. Of particular help is his chapter "The Fight of Faith.")

Fromm, Erich. *The Revolution of Hope: Toward a Humanized Technology*. New York: Harper & Row, 1968. (This is a book on technology. Its aim is to show us how to avoid a completely mechanized society by channeling technique to the service of human well-being. It is an appeal for a "humanized technology.")

Goudzwaard, Bob. *Idols of Our Time*. Trans. by Mark Vander Vennen. Downers Grove, Ill.: Inter-Varsity Press, 1984. (This is a helpful little book in discerning the ideologies that dominate our age. Goudzwaard discusses such ideologies as revolution, nation, material prosperity, and guaranteed security. Well worth the reading.)

Malik, Charles Habib. *A Christian Critique of the University*. Downers Grove, Ill.: Inter-Varsity Press, 1982. (A very helpful statement on one of the most powerful institutions in modern society. He looks at the university as a spiritual power. Few would have the credibility to do what Dr. Malik has done, but he is eminently qualified for this task and does it skillfully.)

Sider, Ronald J., and Richard K. Taylor. *Nuclear Holocaust & Christian Hope: A Book for Christian Peacemakers*. Downers Grove, Ill.: Inter-Varsity Press, 1982. (Discusses militarism as a power. The authors are concerned to utilize peacemaking as an active tool in the Christian arsenal against the powers. This is a significant book, and it should not be neglected.)

Solzhenitsyn, Aleksander I. *The Gulag Archipelago 1918–1956: An Experiment in Literary Investigation*. Trans. by Thomas P. Whitney. New York: Harper & Row, 1973. (If you need to be reminded of the totalitarian depths that the state—any state—can reach, this is the book for you. Solzhenitsyn is clearly one of the most important writers today.)

Wallis, Jim, ed. *Waging Peace: A Handbook for the Struggle to Abolish Nuclear Weapons*. San Francisco: Harper & Row, 1982. (A helpful series of articles by various writers on how to confront militarism. The two significant values in the book are that it treats the issue from a biblical perspective and that it seeks peacemaking as an active and aggressive work.)

POWER AND THE BUSINESS WORLD

Butt, Howard. *The Velvet Covered Brick: Christian Leadership in an Age of Rebellion.* New York: Harper & Row, 1973. (A very helpful book on the questions of authority and submission in the business world. The book arises out of Howard's own experiences as a businessman and the conflicts he faced. He views Christ as possessing both velvet [submission] and brick [authority] and tries to show how both can function in the business world.)

Drucker, Peter F. *The Effective Executive.* New York: Harper & Row, 1966. (A very good and very readable book on the executive task. Drucker develops five major habits essential to the executive: time management, deciding what contribution you should make, how to use your strengths for maximum effect, learning to set right priorities, and effective decision making. Drucker is probably the number one authority on the task of the business executive.)

Fisher, Roger, and William Ury. *Getting to Yes: Negotiating Agreement Without Giving In.* Edited by Bruce Patton. New York: Penguin Books, 1981. (This book is the result of a Harvard study that devised a process called "principled negotiation" that avoids the adversary dilemma without merely giving in. A helpful little book.)

Greenleaf, Robert K. *Servant Leadership: A Journey into the Nature of Legitimate Power and Greatness.* New York: Paulist Press, 1977. (Certainly the best single book on the nature of legitimate power and greatness. Serious Christian thinking underlies this attempt to view corporate institutions as servants.)

Rush, Myron. *Management: A Biblical Approach.* Wheaton, Ill.: Victor Books, 1983. (This book tries to put management principles and practices into a biblical framework.)

Zaleznik, Abraham, and Manfred F. R. Kets de Vries. *Power and the Corporate Mind.* Boston: Houghton Mifflin, 1975. (Brings together three separate modes of analysis—psychology, sociology, and management—in a study of how and why individual executives exercise power. It is a fresh attempt to answer the question, Why does a particular executive function as he or she does?)

108

Foster, Richard J. *Celebration of Discipline.* San Francisco: Harper & Row, 1978. (Contains chapters on submission and service that can help amplify the idea of the vow of service.)

King, Martin Luther, Jr. *Strength to Love.* New York: Pocket Books, 1963. (I include this book because it was among the first of the modern era to help Christians see the connection between their spirituality and social reality. It is a collection of sermons that deal with divine love as the power that overcomes the world.)

McNamara, James. *The Power of Compassion.* New York: Paulist Press, 1983. (A tender little book that underscores the fact that in weakness power reaches perfection. McNamara sees powerlessness as an adversary to true spirituality and shows that it is compassion that can turn power into a force for good.)

McNeill, Donald P., Douglas A. Morrison, and Henri J. M. Nouwen. *Compassion: A Reflection on the Christian Life.* Garden City, N.Y.: Image Books, 1983. (An important book that helps us understand compassion as a force of prayer and action that confronts evil in all its forms. The drawings in the book continually force us to relate the topic of compassion to the contemporary political anguish in South America.)

Moltmann, Jürgen. *The Power of the Powerless.* Trans. by Margaret Kohl. San Francisco: Harper & Row, 1983. (A series of sermons written by a leading theologian. Moltmann helps us to understand the biblical message for powerless people. He examines the usual responses to powerlessness, anger or resignation, finds both deficient, and suggests an alternative manifested in the crucified Christ.)

Nouwen, Henri J. M. *The Wounded Healer.* Garden City, N.Y.: Image Books, 1979. (A tender book that speaks of ministry in terms of suffering love. The point is a simple one: see the suffering of modern society in our own hearts and make that recognition the beginning point for ministry.)

Seifert, Harvey. *Conquest by Suffering: The Process and Prospects of Nonviolent Resistance.* Philadelphia: Westminster Press, 1965. (A study of the power of nonviolent resistance.)

Smedes, Lewis B. *Love Within Limits: A Realist's View of 1 Corinthians 13.* Grand Rapids, Mich.: Eerdmans, 1978. (A very hopeful and realistic look at the power of love based upon 1 Corinthians 13.)

Tournier, Paul. *The Violence Within*. Trans. by Edwin Hudson. San Francisco: Harper & Row, 1978. (In this book Tournier studies the interrelationship between violence and power. He helps us to see that we are a violent people because of our obsession with power. A full seventeen chapters are devoted to analyzing the nature of power in modern society. Tournier also has a helpful chapter on power in an earlier book, *The Whole Person in a Broken World*. Trans. by John and Helen Doberstein, [New York: Harper & Row, 1964].)

Appendix: Sources for Readings

CHAPTER 1

Thomas à Kempis. *The Imitation of Christ*. Trans. by E. M. Blaiklock. London: Hodder & Stoughton, 1979; 2d impression, 1982, p. 29.

Francis Moloney. *A Life of Promise: Poverty, Chastity, Obedience*. Wilmington, Del.: Michael Glazier, 1984, p. 166.

Donald D. McClanen. *Wellspring Newsletter* (15 Feb. 1977), Ministry of Money, 11301 Neelsville Church Road, Germantown, Md.

Thomas Merton. *No Man Is an Island*. New York: Octagon, 1983, p. 173.

Kenneth Leech. *True Prayer*. San Francisco: Harper & Row, 1980, p. 81.

CHAPTER 2

Richard J. Foster. *Freedom of Simplicity*. San Francisco: Harper & Row, 1981, p. 88.

John Woolman. *The Journal of John Woolman*. Secaucus, N.J.: Citadel Press, 1972, p. 168.

Jacques Ellul. *Money & Power*. Downers Grove, Ill.: Inter-Varsity Press, 1984, p. 88.

Herb Goldberg and Robert T. Lewis. *Money Madness*. New York: William Morrow, 1978, pp. 13–14.

Peter H. Davids. "God and Mammon." Part 2. *Sojourners* (March 1978), p. 29.

CHAPTER 3

Edward W. Bauman. *Where Your Treasure Is*. Arlington, Va.: Bauman Bible Telecasts, 1980, p. 127.

Clement of Alexandria. *The Rich Man's Salvation* 16.3.

Andrew Murray. *Money.* Old Tappan, N.J.: Fleming H. Revell, 1897, pp. 10–11.

Stanley Mooneyham. *What Do You Say to a Hungry World?* Waco, Tex.: Word Books, 1975, p. 76.

Robert P. Meye. "The Pastor and Money." *Theology, News and Notes.* Pasadena, Calif.: Fuller Theological Seminary (Dec. 1982), p. 11.

CHAPTER 4

Dietrich Bonhoeffer. *The Cost of Discipleship.* New York: Macmillan, 1963, p. 194.

Richard J. Foster. *Freedom of Simplicity*, p. 128.

John Wesley. Quoted in Edward W. Bauman *Where Your Treasure Is,* p. 159.

George Fooshee, Jr. *You Can Be Financially Free.* Old Tappan, N.J.: Fleming H. Revell, 1980, p. 57.

Virgil Vogt, *Treasure in Heaven: The Biblical Teaching About Money, Finances, and Possessions.* Ann Arbor, Mich.: Servant Books, 1982, p. 97.

CHAPTER 5

Dietrich Bonhoeffer. *The Cost of Discipleship*, p. 197.

François Fénelon. *Christian Perfection.* New York: Harper & Brothers, 1947, p. 194.

Richard J. Foster. *Celebration of Discipline.* San Francisco: Harper & Row, 1978, pp. 78–82.

A. W. Tozer. *The Pursuit of God.* Harrisburg, Penn.: Christian Publications, 1948, p. 27.

E. F. Schumacher. *Less Is More.* Edited by Goldian Vandenbroeck. New York: Harper Colophon Books, 1978, p. xv.

CHAPTER 6

C. S. Lewis. *Mere Christianity.* New York: Macmillan, 1960, p. 91.

Lewis B. Smedes. *Sex for Christians.* Grand Rapids, Mich.: Eerdmans, 1976, p. 42.

James B. Nelson. *Embodiment: An Approach to Sexuality and Christian Theology.* Minneapolis: Augsburg, 1978, p. 50.

H. A. Williams. *Poverty, Chastity & Obedience: The True Virtues.* London: Mitchell Beazley, 1975, pp. 78–79.

Derrick Sherwin Bailey. *The Mystery of Love and Marriage: A Study in the Theology of Sexual Relations.* New York: Harper & Brothers, 1952, pp. 43–44.

CHAPTER 7

Heini Arnold. *In the Image of God: Marriage and Chastity in Christian Life.* Rifton, N.Y.: Plough Publishing House, 1977, p. 161.

C. S. Lewis. *Mere Christianity*, pp. 93–94.

Henri J. M. Nouwen. *Clowning in Rome: Reflection on Solitude, Celibacy, Prayer, and Contemplation.* Garden City, N.Y.: Image Books, 1979, pp. 48–49.

Elisabeth Elliot. *Passion and Purity.* Old Tappan, N.J.: Fleming H. Revell, 1984, p. 21.

Letha Dawson Scanzoni. *Sexuality.* Philadelphia: Westminster Press, 1984, p. 109.

CHAPTER 8

Martin Luther. In Arthur C. McGiffert, *Martin Luther: The Man and His Work.* New York: Century, 1910, pp. 287–88.

C. S. Lewis. *The Four Loves.* New York: Harcourt Brace Jovanovich, 1960, p. 140.

Dietrich Bonhoeffer. *The Cost of Discipleship*, p. 149.

Elizabeth Achtemeier. *The Committed Marriage.* Philadelphia: Westminster Press, 1976, p. 187.

Heini Arnold. *In the Image of God*, pp. 71–72.

CHAPTER 9

Dietrich Bonhoeffer. *The Cost of Discipleship*, pp. 318–19.

C. S. Lewis. *Mere Christianity*, p. 98.

Henri J. M. Nouwen. *Intimacy: Essays in Pastoral Psychology.* San Francisco: Harper & Row, 1969, pp. 31–32.

Charlie Shedd and Martha Shedd. *Celebration in the Bedroom.* Waco, Tex.: Word, 1979, pp. 42–43.

Walter Trobisch. *I Loved A Girl: A Private Correspondence Between Two*

Young Africans and Their Pastor. New York: Harper & Row, 1965, p. 4.

CHAPTER 10

Paul Tournier, *The Violence Within.* Trans. by Edwin Hudson. San Francisco: Harper & Row, 1978, p. 155.

Jacques Ellul. *Violence: Reflections from a Christian Perspective.* New York: Seabury Press, 1969, pp. 163–65.

Hendrik Berkhof. *Christ and the Powers.* Trans. by John H. Yoder. Scottdale, Penn.: Herald Press, 1962, p. 47.

Paul Tournier. *The Whole Person in a Broken World.* Trans. by John and Helen Doberstein. New York: Harper & Row, 1964, p. 136.

Heinrich Schlier. *Principalities and Powers in the New Testament.* Silver Springs, Md.: Herder & Herder, 1961, p. 48.

CHAPTER 11

Paul Tournier. *The Violence Within,* p. 113.

Henri J. M. Nouwen. "Letting Go of All Things." In *Waging Peace,* edited by Jim Wallis. San Francisco: Harper & Row, 1982, p. 200.

Dietrich Bonhoeffer. *The Cost of Discipleship,* p. 189.

Cheryl Forbes. *The Religion of Power.* Grand Rapids, Mich.: Zondervan, 1983, p. 121.

George Fox. *The Journal of George Fox.* Cambridge: Cambridge University Press, 1952, pp. 199–200.

CHAPTER 12

James McNamara. *The Power of Compassion.* New York: Paulist Press, 1983, p. 38.

Gerald Vann. *The Divine Pity.* Garden City, N.Y.: Image Books, 1961, p. 98.

M. Scott Peck. *The Road Less Traveled.* New York: Simon & Schuster, 1978, pp. 284–85.

Paul Tournier. *The Violence Within,* p. 145.

Lewis B. Smedes. *Love Within Limits: A Realist's View of 1 Corinthians 13.* Grand Rapids, Mich.: Eerdmans, 1978, p. 130.

CHAPTER 13

Dietrich Bonhoeffer. *Life Together.* New York: Harper & Row, 1954, p. 99.

Robert K. Greenleaf. *Servant Leadership: A Journey into the Nature of Legitimate Power and Greatness.* New York: Paulist Press, 1977, p. 49.

James Nayler. *Christian Faith and Practice in the Experience of the Society of Friends.* Richmond, Ind.: Friends United Press, 1973; London: London Yearly Meeting of the Religious Society of Friends, 1960, no. 25.

Martin Hengel. *Christ and Power.* Philadelphia: Fortress Press, 1977, p. 27.

Donald P. McNeill, Douglas A. Morrison, and Henri J. M. Nouwen. *Compassion: A Reflection on the Christian Life.* Garden City, N.Y.: Image Books, 1982, p. 24.

Scripture Index

Acts: *1:6-8*, 3; *1:8*, 94; *4:32-37*, 3, 35; *4:34*, 35; *8:9-24*, 3;
   15:1-29, 88; *19:18-20*, 29
Romans: *1:24-32*, 49; *1:26-27*, 50; *12:8*, 34; *12:9-21*, 99;
   12:10, 101; *12:15*, 61
1 Corinthians: *2:6-8*, 83; *4:19-20*, 94; *6:9-10*, 50; *6:15-20*,
   65; *7:3-5*, 60; *7:8-9*, 55; *7:12-16*, 60; *7:25-28*, 55;
   7:32-35, 55; *10:23-24*, 57; *10:31*, 30; *12:8-10*, 82; *13*,
   64, 66; *13:1-7*, 99; *13:8*, 66
2 Corinthians: *8-9*, 24; *8:1-7*, 34; *8:13-15*, 29; *8:14*, 24;
   9:6-12, 23
Galatians: *5:1*, 84, 90; *5:1-15*, 88; *5:13*, 85; *5:19-21*, 3
Ephesians: *1:19-23*, 83; *2:1-2*, 83; *4:31-32*, 55; *5:21-6:9*,
   60, 99; *5:28-33*, 65; *6*, 84; *6:11*, 85; *6:12-18*, 83
Philippians: *2:5-8*, 99; *2:10-11*, 98; *4:6*, 36; *4:8*, 55, 94;
   4:10-13, 34
Colossians: *1:15-20*, 83; *2:8-15*, 83; *2:20-21*, 84; *2:20-23*,
   83; *3:16b*, 36; *3:18-4:1*, 60
1 Timothy: *1:9-10*, 50; *6:6-10*, 3; *6:10*, 19
2 Timothy: *1:7*, 85
Hebrews: *10:24*, 66; *11:35-38*, 88; *12:1*, 95
James: *2:1-9*, 34; *3:6-12*, 94; *4:13-16*, 30
1 John: *1:9*, 5; *2:15-17*, 3, 94; *4:7-14*, 88